The Practical Mariner of Knowledge

420 SEA-TESTED RULES OF THUMB FOR ALMOST EVERY BOATING SITUATION

JOHN VIGOR

INTERNATIONAL MARINE
CAMDEN, MAINE

The McGraw·Hill Companies

12 13 14 15 16 17 18 19 20 DOC DOC 0 9 8 7 6 5 4

Library of Congress Cataloging-in-Publication Data
Vigor, John
   The practical mariner's book of knowledge : 420 sea-tested rules of thumb for almost every boating situation / John Vigor.
      c. cm.
   Includes bibliographical references and index.
   ISBN 0-07-067475-2
   1. Boats and boating. I. Title
GV775.V54   1994
797.1—dc20   93-40390
                                             CIP

Questions regarding the content of this book should be addressed to:
International Marine
P.O. Box 220
Camden, Maine 04843

Questions regarding the ordering of this book should be addressed to:
The McGraw-Hill Companies
Customer Service Department
P.O. Box 547
Blacklick, OH 43004
Retail Customers: 1-800-262-4729
Bookstores: 1-800-722-4726

Printed by R. R. Donnelley, Crawfordsville, IN
Design by James R. Brisson
Production and page layout by Janet Robbins
Edited by Jonathan Eaton, Roger C. Taylor, Kathy Newman

CONTENTS

Topics in **boldface** have multiple entries.

FOREWORD

Thinking back, it was probably about seven years ago now that I made the acquaintance of John Vigor. I had been working late one evening in the editorial offices of *Cruising World*; the phone rang and I picked it up to hear the static of a long-distance connection.

John was calling from his home in South Africa, "out of the blue," he said, to introduce himself and to inquire if by chance *Cruising World* would be interested in seeing any of his writing.

He was an experienced newspaperman, he explained, and an avid sailor. His manner was warm and familiar, the vibes felt right, and shortly thereafter we began receiving the stories of John and June Vigor's entree into the world of cruising.

John's five-part series on the nuts and bolts, preparations, fears, and concerns of how to leave the workaday world and actually go offshore cruising was one of the most inspirational and popular we have ever run in *Cruising World*.

In 1987, the Vigors sailed their 31-footer, *Freelance*, 7,000 miles from Durban, South Africa, transatlantic to the Caribbean, and then up to Florida. But it wasn't until 1991, when we all met finally for lunch here at our offices in Newport, Rhode Island, that John told us the real story of his family's emotional and exciting exodus from their South African homeland.

After some convincing by our editors, John finally agreed to share the story with our readers in what turned out to be a major two-part feature in *Cruising World*.

John's beautifully written and intimate story told of the Vigors' "escape" with their youngest son from the country they loved, but whose politics they could no longer abide.

We received more reader mail on this emotional and exciting series than on almost anything we have ever run in the magazine.

In this new book, *The Practical Mariner's Book of Knowledge*, John is in his element. The 400 plus entries are all amusing and useful, and are woven together in John's rich and witty style.

One in particular—Vigor's Black Box Theory—sticks in my memory as summing up the author himself. The basis of the theory, John says, is that there is no such thing as fortuitous luck at sea. The reason why some boaters survive storms or have fewer accidents than others is that they earn their luck by diligent and constant acts of seamanship.

"Aboard every boat there's an invisible black box," he writes. "Every time a skipper takes the trouble to consult the chart, inspect the filters, go forward on a rainy night to check the running lights, or take any proper seamanlike precaution, he or she earns a point that goes into the black box. In times of stress, in heavy weather or other threatening circumstances where human skill and effort can accomplish no more, the points are cashed in as protection. . . . Those skippers with no points in the box are the ones later described as unlucky."

John knows well about earning points at sea to put in a black box of experiences, for he has had more than most. His gift as a writer is in being able to translate those experiences for the reader with intelligence, humor, and a warmth of spirit. This engaging collection is a testament to that gift, and to one of the finest boating writers at work today.

Bernadette Bernon
Editor, *Cruising World*

ACKNOWLEDGMENTS

I was a schoolboy when I met Bernard Moitessier and Jean Gau. I nearly met Marcel Bardiaux, too, but I was shy and so was he. Twice I stood next to Eric and Susan Hiscock but didn't say a word. These pioneers of ocean voyaging in small boats were my special heroes and still are...they, and Harry Pegram, who trusted me to pilot his sportfisher *Makoti* off Cape Point when I was just 14. They all sparked in me an interest—very well, an obsession—in boats and the sea that has enriched my life and brought me enduring delight and satisfaction.

I also owe a debt of gratitude to many mariners, amateur and professional, who sailed those same deep waters before my heroes and after them. They are, of course, too numerous to mention by name, and in any case I don't know all their names. I know only that the nautical rules of thumb they discovered have helped generations of seafarers and will probably help generations more.

Many of the rules and suggestions listed in this book were culled over decades from the yachting press, specifically from such magazines as *Yachting World*, *Yachting Monthly*, and *Practical Boat Owner* in Britain, and *Cruising World*, *Rudder*, *Practical Sailor*, *Boatbuilder*, and *SAIL* in the United States.

A list of some of the books that proved helpful to me appears in the Bibliography at the end of this book.

INTRODUCTION

Mariners are incurable worriers, and rightly so. It's what keeps us alive. Every one of us, now and then, is seized by a dreadful suspicion that the mast is too thin, the keel bolts too few, or the engine oil too dark for its own good.

With the help of tried and tested rules of thumb—the distilled essence of centuries of seafaring experience—this book sets out to provide succinct answers to most of the questions amateur sailors and powerboaters ask about small boats and the sea.

Is that anchor large enough? Is there sufficient water on board? Why do people steer in circles in the fog?

This wide-ranging and comprehensive book gives quick and easily found answers in basic terms. Many of these rules of thumb have been handed down to us by professional sailors and boatbuilders, and all pay respect to the needs of safe and cautious seamanship.

One ancient rule, and possibly the very one that spawned the phrase, was that a prudent captain should never allow his vessel to come closer to danger than one thumb's width on the chart. By this means, a vessel was kept a fair distance away on a small-scale chart, and brought considerably closer with a more detailed chart. That advice holds good to this day.

Other rules of thumb are more modern. As boatbuilding technology evolves, the strength and longevity of materials such as glass fiber, carbon fiber, synthetic resins, and sailcloth are tested in the ancient manner: by observing and comparing their behavior on vessels at sea. Thus, new rules of thumb are born, so that boaters now know roughly how thick a fiberglass hull should be and how much strain a nylon hawser can take.

Sound, simple advice about boats is surprisingly hard to find, at sea or in harbor. Because boating involves so many different disciplines, the facts one seeks often are scattered among dozens of different volumes. Furthermore, every boater has his or her diverse opinions and is rarely inhibited about sharing them. The beginner, in particular, must necessarily make heavy weather of all these confusing, though well-intentioned, suggestions.

But no matter if you're a newcomer to boating, or halfway through your third singlehanded ocean crossing and wondering how much longer your rickety keel bolts will hold together, you'll find most of the answers in the rules of thumb between these two covers. They spell out what is generally believed to be sane, safe, and reasonable.

There are, in any case, few absolutely precise answers in a boater's world. To be dogmatic is to invite pointless and endless argument, so I have confined myself to passing on suggestions about the gear and techniques that time and use have proved acceptable. There are, after all, still many mysteries concerning the way of a ship in the midst of the sea. And the sea still scoffs at man's cleverest calculations.

There are more than 400 rules of thumb here, set out alphabetically for swift, easy access. If greater accuracy is needed, it will in most cases be found in the handy tables and formulas of the Appendix.

I hope seasoned boaters will enjoy this book as much for entertainment as for information. Many of the manners and rituals of the sea are revealed in rules of thumb such as the one that states that honored guests come aboard from the starboard side, while stores, crew, and tradesmen come aboard from port. And if you've ever wondered what it means when the cocktail party flag is flown upside down...well, the answer's inside.

The Practical Mariner's Book of Knowledge is the fruit of more than 40 years of reading yachting books, tearing pages out of boating magazines, and collecting wise sayings of the sea.

It will please me well if the result proves as fascinating as it is factual.

John Vigor
Oak Harbor, Washington
October 1993

A

Abandoning Ship The rule of thumb is never to abandon ship until you have to step *up* to your liferaft.

Unfortunately, this is much easier said than done. There is often great psychological pressure to escape from the responsibilities, physical labor, decision-making, stress, and sense of failure that accompany a sinking situation in heavy weather. Many sailors suffering mental and physical exhaustion after a knock-down or a holing find the thought of drifting off in a rubber liferaft—and thereby abdicating all decision-making and physical labor—immensely appealing. But, all too often, the partially water-logged yacht is found still floating, months or even years later, while the liferaft and its occupants are never seen again.

Aground *See*: RUNNING AGROUND, FIRST ACTION TO TAKE

Air Pressure, on Sails and Rigging The force applied by wind to a boat's sails, or to its rigging and superstructure while at anchor, varies with the density of the air.

Cold air is denser than is warm air, so a sailboat heels more (with the same sail area and wind speed) in higher latitudes than in the tropics, or more in autumn than in summer.

The force of the wind also increases as a square of its speed, which means that if the wind speed doubles, its force increases four times.

See also: APPENDIX: HORSEPOWER GENERATED BY SAILS, APPROXIMATE; AND APPENDIX: WIND PRESSURE ACCORDING TO WIND SPEED

Albatross, Superstition Concerning

It was widely believed by European mariners that an albatross housed the soul of a dead sailor.

It was therefore very bad luck to kill one, as Samuel Taylor Coleridge tells us in *The Rime of the Ancient Mariner*.

Alternator, Power Absorbed by

It's easy to regard the alternator as a source of free power, just spinning away as the engine runs. But, in fact, it takes a surprising amount of power—and therefore fuel, which could affect a boat's range—to turn over an alternator.

The rule of thumb is that the horsepower drain on the engine is twice the number of kilowatts produced. If, for example, a 100-amp alternator is charging a 12-volt system at full capacity, it's producing 1,200 watts or 1.2 kilowatts. So, it steals 2.4 h.p. from the engine's output.

Alternator, Sizing Rule

Your alternator should have a recharging capacity in amps of between 25 and 40 percent of the total amp-hours in your battery bank.

This presupposes you are using a modern, multi-step regulator that won't allow overcharging, particularly when the batteries become warm. If you don't have a multi-step regulator, the rule of thumb for long battery life is that you should limit the charging rate in amps to 10 percent of available amp-hours. But, because this takes so long, most boaters don't heed this rule, preferring to charge at about 20 to 25 percent and to buy new batteries more frequently as a consequence.

Anchor, Best Type to Use

Once you understand the idiosyncrasies of your particular anchor, you can make it dig in and hold on almost any kind of bottom. However, these are the general characteristics of the more popular types of anchors:

Pivoting plow type (C.Q.R. and others): Good all-rounder, best in sand and mud. Poor on weed and hard rock. Cannot be fouled by its rode. Good at resetting itself when direction of pull is changed.

Fisherman type (Herreshoff, Luke, and others): Better than most on rocky and grassy bottoms, but needs to be heavier than most other anchors and can be fouled and dislodged by its own rode. Small fluke area drags easily through soft bottoms. Awkward to handle, but can be dismantled for stowage.

Lightweight type (Danforth, Fortress, Performance, and others): Sharp points on flukes are good at digging into hard sand and better than most at penetrating grass. Large fluke area is helpful in soft mud. Not good at resetting itself. Has great holding power.

Bruce type: Very strongly built, good all-rounder. A modified plow with no moving parts. Cannot foul itself. Stows conveniently in a bow roller and resets itself well. Good in sand, mud, rock, and coral.

Delta type: A sturdy, one-piece, non-pivoting plow. Weighted to land correctly, penetrate hard bottoms, and set itself quickly. Launches itself easily from bow roller and cannot foul its rode.

Anchor, Fisherman, Ideal Proportions of

The fisherman-type anchor is not widely carried on modern pleasure boats because it's awkward to handle and stow, and because it's easily fouled by its own rode. Newer designs of anchor—such as the Bruce, the C.Q.R., the Danforth, the Delta, and others—have largely eliminated these faults, but the fisherman still has its uses, especially where the bottom is hard, rocky, or covered with grass.

Not all fisherman anchors are created equal, however. Claud Worth, the classic British sailor and author of *Yacht Cruising*, gave this advice for selection:

> The arms and shank should be oval or flat in section. The flukes should be sharp and long to bite into hard ground. They should make an angle of about 40 degrees with the shank. The measurement from the crown to the hole for the stock should be not less than 1½ times, nor more than 1⅔ times, the length of the chord—the chord being the distance between the tips of the two flukes. The stock should be the same length as the shank.

Anchor, Proper Scope

Under favorable weather conditions, the minimum scope of an anchor cable should be 5:1. Under average conditions, a scope of 7:1 is considered satisfactory. As much as 10:1 is needed in heavy weather.

Scope is measured as the ratio between the depth of the water and the length of the anchor cable veered out. Note that the depth of the water in this calculation also includes the extra length between water level and the bow chock. In other words, *depth of water* really means the distance from your bow roller straight down to the sea bed.

These amounts of scope allow a nylon rode with at least 8 feet of chain (preferably more) attached to the anchor to exert a low angle of pull against the anchor. Most anchors tend to break out if the angle of pull is more than 8 degrees from the horizontal.

The temptation to pay out less scope on an all-chain rode should be resisted. Although the catenary of the chain cushions shock loads from large waves, once the slack has been taken up, the snatching loads on your anchor and samson post, or anchor winch, are much greater than they would be with a stretchy nylon rode.

Anchor, Safe Minimum Weight of

Although it's their engineering design that makes them effective, anchors still need weight to dig into the bottom. It's generally agreed that no matter how small a yacht may be, it's not wise to use any anchor weighing less than 30 pounds for any purpose other than temporary halts during which the yacht is adequately manned and ready to sail at short notice.

Anchor, Size of
Owners of cruising yachts should beware of generalized suggestions from anchor manufacturers about the size of anchors they need.

Seventy percent or more of many types of anchors are sold to inland fishermen for use with small open boats on lakes. Understandably, manufacturers' recommendations are tailored to this market, not the market constituting the 2 percent of their customers with offshore voyaging boats.

See also: APPENDIX: ANCHORS, RECOMMENDED SIZES

Anchor, Time Spent at, While Cruising

While cruising in Mexico, the Caribbean, and the South Pacific, the average yacht spends 10 percent of the time at sea, 5 percent tied to docks, and 85 percent at anchor.

This rule of thumb, which originated with Lin and Larry Pardey, points to the importance of good ground tackle and an efficient dinghy.

Anchor, Weight One Person Can Handle

The rule of thumb is that it's possible for a person of average strength and fitness to raise and bring aboard a 60-pound Danforth or C.Q.R. anchor without any special gear.

Nevertheless, it's heavy work, and in boats exceeding 5 or 6 tons of displacement, some mechanical assistance is generally considered necessary. A chain pawl attached at or near the bow roller is of great assistance. It also makes it feasible to do away with an anchor winch or windlass altogether when using a 35-pound anchor and ⁵⁄₁₆ chain, particularly if an auxiliary engine can be used to ease the ship to windward while weighing.

Anchorage, Safe When seeking a safe anchorage, bear in mind these basic requirements:

- Shelter from wind and waves
- Room to swing around the anchor
- Sufficient depth of water at low tide
- Good holding ground for the anchor

Anchor Chain, Bitter End, Securing The inboard or bitter end of the anchor chain should be secured with about three fathoms of appropriately sized nylon line to the base of the samson post, king post, or other heavy structural member in the chain locker.

The nylon line is easier to cast off, or cut and buoy, in the event of the cable having to be slipped quickly. The elasticity of the nylon also helps absorb the considerable shock of a runaway anchor chain coming up short against its bitter-end fastening. A chain shackled internally to a bolt through the bow might simply blast a hole through the hull when it reaches the end of its tether.

See also: CHAIN, STRENGTH OF

Anchor Chain, High-Tensile High-tensile chain is traditionally not recommended for anchor rodes. Although it has a high breaking load, it can fail without warning. Ordinary galvanized steel chain with short oval links is usually specified for pleasure-boat use because it gives visible signs of stretching before breaking.

Anchor Chain, Markings for If you have no other way to judge how much chain you're veering, paint a white mark at least a foot long on the cable every five fathoms (30 feet). All too often, in the absence of some method of measuring, insufficient scope is given, which is the gravest crime in the anchoring laws.

If you have trouble counting the marks as the line is paid out, you could try a system with fewer markings in different colors. That way, you can check at a glance the amount of cable veered.

Anchor Chain, Size of The American Boat and Yacht Council uses windage on the boat as a criterion for selecting chain. It recommends that the chain have a breaking strength to withstand at least five times the normal horizontal load.

To estimate the horizontal load, you need to know the frontal surface area on your boat exposed to the effect of windage. The rule of thumb is to multiply bow height by maximum beam. The result is in square feet. Add ⅔ of that figure to account for spars, rigging, and deck gear. Add the frontal area, in square feet, of anything else, such as a raised dodger. Then double the resulting figure to account for the effects of yawing. The pressure of wind on this square footage varies with its speed.

See also: CHAIN, STRENGTH OF; APPENDIX: CHAIN, RECOMMENDED SIZES FOR ANCHOR; AND APPENDIX: WIND PRESSURE ACCORDING TO WIND SPEED

Anchor Light, Required Size Vessels under 50 meters in length must show an all-round white light that is visible for 2 miles when anchored between dusk and dawn, except in designated "special anchorages."

The 2-mile range is normally reached by a 12-watt electric bulb or a ½-inch wick in a kerosene lantern showing through clear glass.

See also: NAVIGATION LIGHTS, SPECIFICATIONS FOR

Anchor Rode, Minimum Length of The length of anchor rode that a vessel needs obviously depends on the depth of water in which she wants to anchor. However, unless she is too small to stow it, no boat should carry less than 30 fathoms (180 feet) of anchor rode. This is sufficient to keep her safe, in all but exceptional weather, in 25 feet of water.

However, it's vastly preferable in all cases to carry at least 50 fathoms (300 feet) to allow for anchoring in deeper water.

Incidentally, the term *rode* is generally taken to mean all the gear lying between a boat and her anchor—no matter whether it's rope or chain—although in New England and Eastern Canada it refers to a fishing boat's anchor *rope*.

Anchoring, Problems with Coral Heads

When anchored in areas where coral heads are prevalent, a chain rode frequently wraps around one or more heads, dangerously shortening the scope. The general rule is to buoy the chain so that the main part of the rode cannot foul coral. Usually, several buoys are needed.

Some experienced cruisers prefer to anchor in depths of between 90 and 120 feet when possible, because coral heads are far less common in deeper water. But this requires more anchor line than many small cruisers can comfortably carry.

Anchoring, Problems with Snatching

In shallow water and steep waves, any boat can snatch badly at her anchor rode. In such circumstances, it's easier on the gear to use a nylon anchor rode to absorb the snatching loads. Even with an all-chain rode, a 20-foot spring of three-strand nylon made fast with a rolling hitch to the chain near the bow is probably more effective than is a traveler weight in preventing destructive snubbing.

Anchoring, Rights of First to Anchor

Long-established nautical custom gives the first boat to anchor in any area the right to ask others not only to give her room to swing freely, but also not to hinder her maneuvering room should she wish to depart. But if there appears to be too little room, the first-anchored yacht *must* inform the newcomer of the possibility of fouling.

The U.S. Admiralty Court upheld the legality of this claim. Decision No. 124-5861 of 1956 states, *inter alia*, that: "A vessel shall be found at fault if it...anchors so close to another vessel as to foul her when swinging...(and/or) fails to shift anchorage when dragging dangerously close to another anchored vessel. Furthermore, the vessel that anchored first shall warn the one who anchored last that the berth chosen will foul the former's berth."

A

9

Anchoring Rights, Restriction of It's an

unfortunate rule of thumb that where states and localities see the opportunity to restrict the anchoring rights of cruising sailors and powerboaters, they will.

Article X of the U.S. Constitution guarantees boaters' rights to navigate freely for the purposes of transportation, commerce, and recreation. Admiralty law has laid down that anchoring is an inseparable part of navigation.

The Submerged Lands Act of 1953, however, gave states ownership of submerged lands from the high tide mark to the 3-mile coastal limit.

The intent of this act was to establish mineral rights and protect natural resources. It strictly prohibits states from regulating navigation. Yet many cities and states believe they have the right, through their inherent police powers, to regulate boating activities in "their" waters.

A rash of anti-anchoring legislation—with penalties of as much as $10,000 a day—particularly in warm-weather states, has led to increasing protest from recreational boaters concerned at this loss of traditional rights.

The fight is likely to be long and drawn out. Ultimately, it will be resolved either by new legislation from Congress or a decision in federal court.

Anchors, Kedge and Bower
By ancient tradition, the bower is a ship's principal anchor. The kedge is a smaller anchor, often used in conjunction with the bower but sometimes alone.

For some reason, even self-styled boating authorities habitually confuse the kedge's construction with its size and purpose, maintaining that the kedge is the traditional yachtsman's or fisherman's anchor with arms, flukes, and stocks. It could be, of course, but not necessarily. I can do no better than to quote from Eric Hiscock's classic, *Cruising Under Sail*:

> *Kedge. An anchor smaller than the bower,*
> *often used with a fiber cable instead of a chain.*
> *Used for hauling a vessel off when she has*
> *gone aground and to prevent her from fouling*
> *her bower.*

Traditionally, the kedge is about two-thirds the weight of the bower. Every boat capable of going to sea should carry at least these two anchors. The best prepared of yachts also carries a storm anchor, usually a collapsible fisherman type weighing about twice as much as the bower, that can be stowed low in the boat.

The word *kedge* can also be used as a verb, of course. Kedging off a sandbank is accomplished by sending out the kedge anchor, hauling up to it and repeating the operation as many times as necessary.

Angles, Horizontal, Estimating
With your hand held up at arm's length, these are the approximate angles covered:

20 degrees: Full handspan, thumb tip to little fingertip

15 degrees: Closed fist with extended thumb

10 degrees: Width of closed fist

3 degrees: Thumb's width

2 degrees: Little finger's width

Atoll Passes, Current Movement In

In French Polynesia and the mid-Pacific islands it's difficult to know which way the current will be flowing through atoll passes at any given time. The rule of thumb is that when the moon is directly over your head, or directly under your feet, the current will be slack. A nautical almanac will help you calculate the midpoint between moonrise and moonset (or vice versa) on your meridian.

A

11

B

Balanced Helm, Factors Affecting Monohull Sailboats

On an average deep-keeled hull, weather helm is caused by:

- Excessive beam, especially beam carried far aft
- Mast raked, or positioned, too far aft
- Full-cut sails
- Asymmetrical heeled hull shape
- Heeled center of effort moving to leeward

Lee helm is caused by:

- Mast raked, or positioned, too far forward
- Flat-cut sails

Of course, another set of factors comes into play in a centerboarder or other vessel where the center of lateral resistance of the hull can be altered at will. (*See also*: GRIPING, CAUSES OF; WEATHER HELM, BENEFITS OF)

C. A. Marchaj, a world-renowned naval architect and independent aerodynamic and research scientist, quotes J. Laurent Giles, a prominent British designer, in this fine definition of what constitutes a balanced hull: Good balance, he says, is "freedom from objectionable tendencies to gripe or fall off the wind regardless of angle of heel, speed, or direction of wind."

In his design philosophy, Laurent Giles required that a yacht have "the utmost docility and sureness of maneuvering at sea, in good or bad weather."

Furthermore, he tried to design yachts that would maintain a steady course when left to their own devices, but respond instantly to the helm in heavy weather when there might be large seas to dodge.

Most importantly, in my view, he also stressed that only a properly balanced yacht is capable of being left to her own devices, sailing, hove-to, or under bare poles.

Marchaj states quite bluntly: "Seaworthiness cannot be achieved if the boat is badly balanced."

Ballast and Bad Luck
The ancient rule of thumb stated that the ballast for sailing ships should never be taken from the sea bed.

It made sense. If Davy Jones (otherwise known as the devil) ever wanted his property back, he might claim the whole vessel and crew along with it.

Ballast Ratios, Safe, for Monohulls

Cruising boats: From 30 percent to 40 percent of total displacement

Racing boats: From 40 to 50 percent of displacement

Extreme types, such as the Twelve Meter racing class: As high as 70 percent of displacement

Barometer, Conventional Wisdom Concerning
A yacht's barometer is the simplest and most reliable aid to forecasting local weather.

The accuracy of readings is of less importance than knowledge of whether the air pressure is rising or falling, and how quickly any change is manifesting itself. A recording barograph gives a clear picture of this in graphic form, and is therefore a most valuable forecasting tool. Alternatively, pressures may be (and should be) noted at the end of each four-hour watch and plotted on graph paper if necessary.

In the middle latitudes, a *high* barometer reads about 30.50 inches (1033 millibars); a *low* barometer reads 29.50 inches (999 millibars). The average reading at sea level is 29.9 inches (1013 millibars). Incidentally, 3.4 millibars equal 1/10 inch.

Steady, persistent decrease in pressure: Foul weather is on the way

Steady, persistent increase in pressure: Stabilization of the weather

Unchanging pressure: Fair weather will continue

Sudden rise or sudden fall in pressure: Warning of unsettled weather to come

See also: APPENDIX: WEATHER PROVERBS

Barometer, Diurnal Variation Atmospheric pressure undergoes regular daily changes regardless of local weather patterns. It varies most at the equator, where it rises and falls about 0.15 inch (about 5 millibars), and is almost non-existent in polar regions. Here are the approximate times of fluctuations:

Diurnal rises

Between 4 AM and 10 AM

Between 4 PM and 10 PM

Diurnal falls

Between 10 AM and 4 PM

Between 10 PM and 4 AM

Battens, Sail, Eliminating Eliminating battens from a cruising mainsail can increase the sail's life up to 50 percent.

Sailmakers confirm that battens add considerably to the maintenance costs of any sail. Short battens crease and bend the cloth just forward of the pocket, where persistent chafe and flexing wear out the sailcloth. Full-length battens put considerable stress on the leech and luff ends of their pockets.

Many voyagers choose mainsails with slightly hollow leeches, cut just as genoa headsails are cut. The sail clears the backstay more easily when gybing, and the loss of area in the roach affects a cruising boat mainly on the reach or run, when other sails often can be set in addition if desired.

Batteries, House and Engine, Starting

Batteries sold for use in cars are not recommended for use aboard boats because they are intended to be charged and discharged differently.

If possible, you should have separate marine batteries for starting your motor and running all other equipment. Your starter battery is specially designed to deliver a lot of power for a short period. The assumption is that it will be charged again immediately by the engine's alternator.

Your house battery is designed to deliver less power over much longer periods and should be of the deep-cycle variety—that is, designed to be discharged much more deeply over a much longer period before recharging.

Marine batteries cost considerably more than automotive batteries, but not for the reasons that usually spring to a boater's mind: namely, that anything with the tag "marine" on it automatically assumes an inflated price. The truth is, marine batteries have to be built more ruggedly because they work so much harder for a living—and usually in atrocious conditions.

Batteries, Location of

Batteries are a problem to place in a boat. Because of their great weight, they need to be kept low to maintain the boat's stability. But they also need to be located as high as possible to avoid bilge water and engine heat, and to be accessible.

Batteries need to be protected from extreme cold, salt spray, and hot sunshine. They need to be in an area that is well ventilated so that explosive gas generated during charging dissipates quickly. Because of their propensity to make sparks, batteries should be kept well away from areas where cooking gas or gasoline fumes can collect. They must be securely fastened so they don't shift when the boat heels (or turns turtle), and they must be kept in a container that is proof against acid spills. Those batteries used to start engines must be located as close as possible to the starter motor. And, on top of everything else, they need to be available for easy inspection, testing, and topping up with distilled water. Good luck.

Battery, Power Drawn by Starter Motor

An engine's starter motor draws a very heavy load from the battery, often the equivalent of 7 h.p. or more.

The starter motor for an average, yacht-sized diesel engine with four cylinders or more draws between 300 and 600 amps.

The draw for a similar-sized gasoline engine is between 100 and 300 amps. Of course, these large loads usually are drawn for a few seconds only.

Many batteries specify their cold-cranking ampere (CCA) capacity (technically, the amperage the battery delivers at a temperature of 0 degrees F for a period of 30 seconds without individual cell voltage falling below 1.2).

How many CCAs do you need for your motor? The rule of thumb for diesel engines is to allow 2 CCAs for every cubic inch of your engine's displacement. For gasoline engines, allow 1 CCA per cubic inch.

Battery Capacity Needed It's easy, but tedious, to calculate the battery capacity you need on a boat. Just note the number of watts each DC electrical item draws, not forgetting such items as the starter motor, which draws a lot of amperage for a very short time. If an item is rated in amps instead of in watts, simply convert to watts by multiplying the number of amps by the battery voltage.

For each item, multiply the watts by the number of hours, or portions of an hour, it is in use every day. Each answer is in watt hours. Add up your list of watt hours. Now divide the total by the battery voltage to give you amp hours. Batteries are marked with their capacity in amp hours, so you now know how big a battery, or how many batteries, to buy.

But the rule of thumb is that *usable* battery capacity is 40 percent of total capacity. And your alternator or generator should be suitably rated to replace your total battery capacity, not just your anticipated draw.

See also: APPENDIX: BATTERY CAPACITY, CALCULATION OF NEEDS

Beam, Proportion to Length In ancient times, ships were generally about three times as long as they were broad. However, the longer the vessel, the less beam she needs because stability increases rapidly with length. Many modern monohull pleasure boats have a beam-to-length ratio greater than 3:1, which gives them good initial stability, along with a jerky, tiring movement in a cross sea. However, it's *ultimate* stability that determines whether a boat can right herself after a 180-degree capsize—and that derives not so much from beam (in fact, excessive beam is a handicap) as from adequate ballast correctly placed, a low center of gravity with a long arm of leverage around the center of buoyancy, and, to a certain extent, the shape of the hull and cabintop when immersed.

Bearing, Collision Because sailboats are mostly invisible to radar transmissions from large ships, and because most small boats' navigation lights are almost invisible, it behooves the small boat on the open ocean to keep out of the big ship's way, especially at night.

To determine whether you should change course,

take a compass bearing immediately when you sight the ship on the horizon. If you're going to pass clear, the bearing will change substantially—5 degrees or more—within a few minutes.

If it doesn't change, or changes very slowly, you're probably on a collision course. Make a substantial change of course—60 degrees or more—and hold it until the danger is past.

Don't make the mistake of taking a relative bearing by sighting the ship over a stanchion or some part of your boat's superstructure. It's not a true relative bearing. If your boat wanders off course, the relative bearing changes accordingly, and the false reading might mislead you into thinking you're safe.

If possible, use a hand-bearing compass to give you a bearing. If you *must* use a stanchion instead of a pelorus, be sure your boat is on the same heading every time—check the steering compass.

And, of course, take collision bearings by day as well as by night.

Bearing, Definition of

A bearing is the direction of an object as measured from the observer.

Thus, if you're sinking in a position 10 miles southwest of an oil island, you could be sitting in your liferaft longer than you anticipated if you accidentally indicate in your Mayday call to the Coast Guard that the oil island is bearing southwest. This may seem so elementary as not to warrant discussion but in fact it's easy to make this mistake under stress.

You must make it quite plain. Either say: "Oil island Sierra is bearing northeast, 10 miles," or "My position is 10 miles southwest of oil island Sierra."

Berths, Dimensions of

The minimum length for an adult berth (unless custom designed) is 6 feet 4 inches. The width should be not less than 20 inches.

For greater comfort, 6 feet 6 inches and 24 to 28

inches is the rule of thumb. At sea, a 21-inch-wide berth provides support against too much rolling around. A berth cannot be too wide for sleeping comfort in harbor, however, although it can be too wide for comfortable seating if it doubles as a settee. The minimum width for a comfortable double berth is 44 inches. The mattress for a double berth is best split in two down the middle. For use at sea, a lee-cloth can be brought up between the mattresses and made fast overhead.

Bilge Pumps, Minimum Requirements

No matter how many mechanical or electrical bilge pumps a seagoing boat might carry, she needs a minimum of two manual pumps besides.

They must be placed where they can be worked easily in heavy weather, and the lower ends of the suction pipes must be flexible and fitted with strainers in the form of strum boxes perforated with small holes. The strum boxes must be easily accessible for frequent cleaning.

Don't expect too much from manual pumps. You'd be lucky to pump 15 gallons per minute for an extended period, and it takes only a very small hole or crack to admit that much water.

In an emergency, don't forget that your toilet pump might also act as a bilge pump, and the engine cooling water could be drawn from the bilges, too, with appropriate precautions.

Binoculars, Basic Rule

Every boat should carry two pairs of binoculars: a good pair for your use only, and another very cheap pair for the idiot visitors who keep changing the focus and won't put the strap around their necks.

Binoculars, Best for Boats

The classic yacht size is 7 x 50.

The first figure is the magnification, the second the diameter of the front lenses, which affects the amount of light gathered. Any greater magnification makes visibility difficult because of exaggerated motion on a small yacht. The larger the second figure, the better you'll see in poor light. Incidentally, what most of us call a *pair* of binoculars is a *binocular* to the purist—meaning one instrument with two eyepieces.

Black Box Theory, Vigor's

The basis of the theory is that there is no such thing as fortuitous luck at sea. The reason why some boaters survive storms or have fewer accidents than others is that they *earn* their "luck" by diligent and constant acts of seamanship.

Aboard every boat there's an invisible black box. Every time a skipper takes the trouble to consult the chart, inspect the filters, go forward on a rainy night to check the running lights, or take any proper seamanlike precaution, he or she earns a point that goes into the black box.

In times of stress, in heavy weather or other threatening circumstances where human skill and effort can accomplish no more, the points are cashed in as protection. The skipper has no control over their withdrawal. They withdraw themselves, as appropriate. Those skippers with no points in the box are the ones later described as "unlucky." Those with points to spend will survive—but they must start immediately to replenish their savings, for the sea offers no credit.

This method of "earning luck" was well known in practice, if not in theory, to sailors in square-riggers, who were told:

> *For six days shalt thou labor and do all thou art able;*
>
> *And on the seventh, holystone the decks and scrape the cable.*

Blistering of Fiberglass Hulls

Of all the words that instill fear in the hearts and minds of brave mariners, *blistering* tops the list as far as owners of fiberglass boats are concerned. Osmotic blistering of the hull, or *boat pox*, often is viewed in the same light as bubonic plague or a diagnosis of terminal cancer. But because the causes of blistering are many and varied, so too are the results and the cures. Blistering can be no more than a minor nuisance. It can also be a death sentence. There is just one rule of thumb about blistering—if you ignore it, it will get worse. Something must be done about it, and the sooner the better.

Blisters are usually found in the outer $\frac{1}{10}$ inch of the fiberglass laminate and are caused by the migration of water or water vapor through the gelcoat into the laminate. There it expands the laminate until it pops up in the form of blisters.

One in four boats can be expected to blister in its lifetime, though fewer problems are being experienced with new boats as our knowledge of blister prevention grows.

As soon as you notice blistering, seek expert advice. A slight case might involve no more than sanding down and recoating. But once a hull is severely blistered, the gelcoat and affected laminates must be removed. Then, after the hull has been allowed to dry out, the laminate must be replaced.

The cost? Circumstances vary so much individually that there's no one formula for estimating the cost of repairs. But peeling off the gelcoat and laminates, and rebuilding with vinylester resin laminate and top coating, is a very expensive business that could easily cost 25 percent or more of the value of a fairly new boat, or 50 to 75 percent of the value of an old one.

Blocks, Size of For fiber rope, the sheave diameter should be at least 8 times the rope diameter. For wire rope, the sheave diameter should be at least 20 times the wire diameter, and preferably 40 times.

This ensures easy rendering of the line, avoids

concentration of undue stresses on the sheave, and obviates the premature wear occasioned by over-sharp turns.

Boarding Ladder, Side for According to the old rules of etiquette, the boarding ladder for important visitors should be slung from the starboard side, the *superior* side of the yacht. Provisions, fuel, crew, and tradesmen come aboard from port. The courtesy flag of a foreign nation is flown from the starboard spreader as a sign of respect. And there's a sound reason for swimming from the starboard side of the boat when the head is to port.

Boat, Choosing the Right One for You The right boat for you is the one that makes your favorite on-the-water activity easy.

All boats are compromises. While you can swim, or dive, or fish from most boats, some are better suited to these particular activities than others. No boat will make you happy all of the time. A boat designed to cross oceans may seem very slow and unglamorous compared to the flashy weekend gin palaces that skitter around in close proximity to the fashionable yacht harbors. The best you can hope for is an honest boat that suits your needs and pleases you most of the time.

Boat, Definition of Despite what the wharfside experts tell you, there is no precise definition of the word *boat*.

It's definitely smaller than a ship, but how much? Some cite the dividing line of 20 meters (65.7 feet) overall length used in the International Collision Regulations, which seems reasonable. Others say a boat is a vessel that can be carried aboard a ship. But that's not much help because the bigger the ship, the bigger the boat she can carry. So the arguments continue.

Boom, Metal, Recommended Minimum Sizes

Simple round aluminum:

Diameter: ⅟₄₅ of overall length

Wall thickness: ⅟₂₆ of diameter

Elliptical section booms:

Width (transverse section): ⅟₅₀ of length

Height (vertical section): 1½ times width

Wall: ⅟₂₆ of width

Always round *up* to the nearest fraction of an inch.

Bosun's Chair, Safe Use of
There's one good rule of thumb about working with a bosun's chair: If you fall, it's your own fault.

No matter who is tailing the halyard that's hoisting you up the mast, don't trust them. Take hold of passing shrouds with a vise-like grip. Ease yourself over the spreaders without losing your grip on something that will save you if you slip. Clip your safety line on and off as you go up or down, and don't let anyone hurry you. It's nice to have help to get up that mast, but you're really on your own up there.

Don't take anything for granted, especially the snap shackle that fastens the sail to the halyard. Replace it with an oversized galvanized shackle and screw the pin up tight. Or use two separate lengths of honest-to-goodness light line to join the bosun's chair to the halyard.

When you're up there, be careful not to let any tools fall. Crews on deck don't like that. It pays to tie the most commonly used tools to their bucket with a length of light line. A large loop in the end of each line will enable you to free the tool quickly if the line is getting tangled with your work.

I prefer an ordinary wooden plank with stout lines passing underneath it and the apex of the bridle at chest level. I use a bucket on a separate halyard to contain tools and equipment and lower it to the deck before I start down.

Other people prefer fabric chairs with built-in pockets for tools and low backs that add a slight feeling of security. I prefer to remain insecure and terrified on the theory that if I don't feel complacent, I won't relax my guard.

Singlehanders sometimes attach heavy weights, such as plastic containers filled with water, to the halyard and haul it up the mast. They then attach themselves to the halyard and let the weight of the containers help haul them up the mast.

If you ever have to do this, make sure you weigh more than the water containers or you may ascend to the masthead at high speed and be stuck up there forever. Secure the containers firmly to the halyard because if they come loose you could fall. Don't step straight out of your bosun's chair onto the deck, otherwise you'll have several heavy water containers descending on your head. And make sure the containers can't get hooked up on the spreaders or jammed in the angle of two shrouds, or you could be stuck halfway up until somebody happens along to free you.

Bottom Painting, Golden Rule Attack marine growths on the bottom of your boat immediately after haulout. *Do not* let the bottom get dry before you start scraping.

Weed, slime, and barnacles will harden and become infinitely more difficult to remove if you let them dry on the hull. So use your brushes, scrapers, or high-pressure water jets as soon as you can get to them. Use a hose or a bucket to keep the unscraped hull wet until all growth has been removed. Then let it dry well before painting with antifouling paint.

Breakers, Spilling and Plunging
On the open ocean it's usually breaking waves that cause capsize. So the rule of thumb for all kinds of boats is to avoid breaking waves. But this isn't always possible. The next best thing is to meet such waves end-on. A small boat that gets broadside-on to a large breaking wave is likely to capsize.

B

25

When the wind pumps too much energy into a wave system in too short a period of time, or when a strong current flows contrary to the direction of the waves, or when the bottom of a wave form is hindered by friction against the sea floor, the crest of the wave must get rid of the excess energy by *breaking*, or spilling over.

It can spill over very suddenly and with great energy, as happens when swells turn into surf on a steeply shelving beach. This kind of spillage is termed a *plunging breaker*. Or the crest can spill over more gently, toppling over and running down the face of the swell with little added speed. This is a *spilling breaker* and (luckily) by far the most common on the open ocean.

At sea, plunging breakers, such as those caused by wind against tide or against leftover swell, are very dangerous. The speed of the water in what is known as the *jet* of a plunging breaker can be as much as four times the speed of the advancing wave. Plunging breakers are fairly common in some areas where tidal streams or ocean currents meet sudden gales from the opposite direction.

Shallow water often produces overfalls when tide and wind are opposed, but the depth of the water limits the size of the waves, and thus the danger they can cause.

Incidentally, it's physically impossible for a wave to remain stable in form when its face exceeds a steepness ratio of 1 in 7. After that, it must either spill or plunge.

Brightwork *See*: VARNISH (multiple entries)

Bulwarks, Depth of Bulwarks are a great comfort and safety factor on a small cruising sailboat. They prevent gear and sails from sliding overboard, and they provide better protection than do toerails against a foot slipping over the edge of a heeled deck. They also provide much firmer anchorage for lifeline stanchions and, when correctly proportioned, can be used to alter the sheerline.

Almost any depth of bulwark is better than an aluminum toerail as used on racing boats, but it's hardly worth bothering with them if they're less than 3 inches deep. Some experienced voyagers, including Lin and Larry Pardey, advocate much higher bulwarks. The Pardeys admit they're addicted to 8-inch bulwarks on a 29-foot boat, but anything over 4 inches is a great asset.

Buoyage *See*: RED RIGHT RETURNING

Buoys, Effect of Color At sea, the color of a buoy is usually recognizable long before its shape.

Research indicates that red buoys are generally much easier to spot from afar than are green buoys. Green buoys often tend to look black at a distance. At night, buoys with green lights at long range mostly look yellowish at first. Buoys with white lights often appear faintly red at first. These changes are caused by the filtering effect of the atmosphere.

Buoyancy, Center of

Sailboats and displacement powerboats: Usually about 55 percent of the waterline aft of the bow

Most other powerboats: About 60 percent aft of the bow

Buys-Ballot's Law Here's a quick and easy way to determine where the center of an approaching depression lies, so that you can take action to avoid it. Buys-Ballot's law states that if you face the wind in the Northern Hemisphere, the low atmospheric pressure is on your right hand. South of the equator, low pressure is on your left hand when you face the wind, and barometric pressure increases on your right hand.

B

27

C

**Capsize, Avoidance Techniques for Sail-
boats** In very heavy weather, the rule of thumb is
that a boat with a long, traditional type of keel is
more resistant to capsize when not making way
through the water than is a hull with a high
aspect–ratio fin keel.

A yacht at sea is a dynamic system that receives
overturning energy from waves. A traditional keel
and hull shape are effective at dissipating this
energy gradually—absorbing the blows of the seas,
as it were. A fin-keel boat has far less area in which
to pass on the energy to the sea, and is more vulnerable to capsize when lying still in the water. But a
fin-keeler becomes more resistant to capsize when
she is kept moving and can thus dissipate the incoming wave energy into a greater area of water. A traditional cruising boat, having a more effective roll-
damping keel, can better look after herself when
lying almost still in the water, ahull or hove-to.

C. A. (Tony) Marchaj, a small-boat sailor who is
also an internationally renowned aerodynamic and
research scientist, is of the opinion that the keel of
a truly seaworthy boat should be designed primarily for the survival situation—that is, zero speed—
which implies a traditional keel with large lateral
area and depth of the hull underbody.

In his book *Seaworthiness: The Forgotten Factor*,
Marchaj quotes a former editor of *Rudder* magazine,
T. F. Day, who crossed the Atlantic in the 25-foot
yawl *Seabird* in 1911:

*My long experience in small boats has taught
me this: that if a boat is a good boat, when real
trouble comes she is best left alone. She knows
better what to do than you, and if you leave her
alone, she will do the right things, whereas
nine times out of ten you will do the wrong.*

Capsize Screening Formula

That there is inherent danger in excessive beam combined with light displacement was amply demonstrated during the infamous Fastnet Race in Britain in 1979, when about half the fleet of ocean-going racers suffered knockdowns or capsizes.

The United States Yacht Racing Union (now the U.S. Sailing Association) subsequently developed a simple rule of thumb known as the Capsize Screening Formula. It gives a rough indication of a sailing yacht's initial resistance to capsizing.

Work out the boat's displacement in cubic feet—that is, divide her displacement in pounds by 64. Then find the cube root of this number. Next, take the boat's beam in feet and tenths of a foot and divide it by the cube root you have just obtained. Normal resistance to capsize is indicated by an answer of 2 or less.

Of course, one must always be aware of the difference between initial stability, in which beam plays a helpful role, and ultimate stability (or ability to recover from an upside-down position) in which excessive beam may be detrimental.

See also: BEAM, PROPORTION TO LENGTH

Carbon Monoxide, Dangers of

The invisible and odorless gas called carbon monoxide has an extraordinary ability to dissipate itself quickly through the atmosphere. It can even travel "uphill" against a steady stream of fresh air.

This tendency makes it a killer aboard a poorly ventilated boat. It's found in engine exhaust gases,

C

29

which can be sucked into the boat over the transom, and it's a product of the combustion of many cooking and heating fuels.

Your best defense is vented stoves, good ventilation, and the knowledge that in the early stages of carbon monoxide poisoning you might feel unnaturally sleepy and headachy.

A battery-operated alarm that warns of the presence of carbon monoxide is available from boat chandlers.

Carrying Capacity, Boats under 20 Feet Overall
A small craft's ability to carry people obviously depends on many things, including the amount of freeboard and her hull shape. However, this simple rule of thumb serves as a guide for an average design:

The maximum number of adults carried should equal overall length times overall beam, in feet, divided by 15. The answer can be rounded up to the nearest whole number. Clearly, as all boats are different, and as some people are bigger than others, this rule should be used with a liberal application of common sense.

Castaways, Survival Rate of
Statistics gathered by the French scientist and adventurer Dr. Alain Bombard show that 9 out of 10 castaways adrift at sea die within three days.

"Yet it takes longer than that to perish of hunger and thirst," he pointed out.

Studies indicate that panic and loss of morale are the chief causes of death. Both may be reduced substantially, however, by careful preparation, mental and physical, for being cast away.

See also: PLANKTON, AS SURVIVAL FOOD

Center of Effort, Position of
An old rule of thumb is that the center of effort (CE) of a sailplan should be 2 to 8 percent of the load waterline length (LWL) forward of the center of lateral resistance (CLR). This is the amount of *lead*.

However, the CE is no more than a theoretical concept useful in planning, designing, and comparison. With a new design, experimentation is most frequently necessary to determine more finely the position and cut of the sails for best hull balance.

Center of Lateral Resistance, Position of

The CLR of a normal cruising hull lies aft of the center of effort of the sailplan by 2 to 8 percent of the load waterline length.

The CLR can most easily be established by balancing a cardboard cutout of the underwater portion of the hull, including the rudder and centerboard if any, on a knife placed at right angles to the fore-and-aft line of the hull. Like the CE, the CLR is merely a handy reference point from which to begin more detailed calculations. Neither is scientifically accurate. In fact, placing the CE ahead of the CLR would logically cause harmful lee-helm; but when the ship has way on, the fore part of the keel is moving in water less disturbed than the after part, so the CLR moves forward.

Chain, Strength of
The only way you can tell the real breaking strength of a length of chain is by testing it to destruction. Therefore, it's customary to consider the safe working load of the chain to be its real strength. The safe working load is one quarter of its theoretical breaking strength.

Proof testing is done by exerting a pull of twice a chain's safe working load—or half the theoretical breaking strength—and inspecting it closely for evidence of elongation or cracking.

See also: ANCHOR CHAIN, HIGH-TENSILE AND ANCHOR CHAIN, SIZE OF

Chain Locker, Estimating Size of
Here is an old method for estimating the size of a locker needed for self-stowing chain. The volume in cubic feet equals the number of fathoms of chain times the

chain size in inches squared, all divided by 2. Multiply the answer by 1.7.

Chart Table, Size of
The minimum size for a chart table in even the smallest vessel is 28 inches by 21 inches.

Ideally, a chart table should measure 28 inches by 42 inches and accept an open standard British Admiralty chart. Incidentally, 100 such charts, folded in the normal manner, fill a 28-inch by 21-inch chart drawer to a depth of 2 inches.

Charts, Scale of
If you, too, have trouble remembering which is which, remember this: Large scale, large detail; small scale, small detail. The scale of a chart indicates a ratio—for instance, a ratio of 1:50,000 means that one inch (or one foot) on the chart represents 50,000 inches (or feet) on the earth's surface. A large-scale chart is one that covers a smaller area with greater detail. A small-scale chart covers a larger area with less detail. Here are some different scales with their uses:

1: 600,000 and smaller: Sailing charts for offshore navigation or voyage planning

1: 150,000 to 1: 600,000: General charts for coastwise navigation

1: 50,000 to 1: 150,000: Coast charts for inshore coastal navigation

1: 50,000 and larger: Harbor charts, for navigation in harbors and on inland waterways

Charts, Stowage of
Unless you're a masochist, your charts should be folded to the size of your chart table and stowed flat. Don't roll them and stow them in tubes. That way lies madness. If there's no other flat stowage, keep them under the skipper's mattress, where they'll be ironed flat while he or she sleeps.

Chartwork, Best Pencil for
From long experience, it has been established that the best pencil for chartwork is one with a medium lead. A No. 2 works well.

A softer pencil makes a bolder line and usually erases more easily, but in the meantime tends to smudge and spread untidily. A harder pencil makes a line that is more difficult to see and more difficult to erase. It also digs too deeply into the chart and shortens its useful life. And don't forget a good eraser—one of the navigator's best friends.

Circles of Position Two leading marks in line form a transit bearing, or range. But it's fascinating to note that if you open up a small angle between the two marks, and keep that angle constant, your course will form an arc of a circle.

C

33

After pre-plotting such a circle of position on a chart, you can place yourself on it accurately merely by keeping constant the correct angle between your leading marks.

Thus, you could use two off-lying islands as marks to keep you clear of hazards while rounding a point of land. A simple way to do this is described by Leonard Eyges in his excellent book *The Practical Pilot: Coastal Navigation by Eye, Intuition, and Common Sense*.

Circling, Accidental Without a compass in fog or dense rain, most helmsmen tend to circle in a clockwise direction.

Well-documented studies carried out in the Northern Hemisphere show that people cut off from sensory information about their surroundings tend to move in a circle, usually clockwise. It doesn't matter whether you're driving a car, walking, swimming, or steering a yacht.

Unfortunately, I have no knowledge of any similar studies from the Southern Hemisphere, so I don't know whether or not the water-down-the-plughole rule applies here. The Northern Hemisphere studies also appear to lack a breakdown of figures into left-handers and right-handers.

Be warned, therefore, that if you are a left-hander circling in a fog south of the equator, you might not be as likely as a right-hander circling in fog in the Northern Hemisphere to be circling in a clockwise direction. I hope this helps.

Circumnavigation, Definition of

The rule of thumb is that the route of a true circumnavigation must encompass two points opposite each other on the surface of the globe. These are points that could be joined by an imaginary straight line passing through the center of the earth.

By definition, the word *circumnavigation* also means a journey "around" the Earth, and thus rules out a voyage whose course merely runs from one of these points, to the other, and back along the reciprocal route.

Cleats, Angle of Pull

Wherever possible, a cleat should be fastened at an angle of about 15 degrees to the direction of the line's pull.

Cleats, Size of

The length of a cleat should be at least 12 times, and preferably 16 times, the diameter of the rope used with it.

This sensible old formula incorporates a safety factor against the rope's slipping or jamming, but regrettably is often ignored in the interests of economy on modern yachts.

Clouds, Walls of, on the Horizon

Towering walls of cloud on the horizon are often an optical illusion and as a rule are less menacing than they appear to be.

This phenomenon is frequently seen in trade-wind seas dotted with puffs of white cumulus. Since we have no way of knowing the true size of the clouds, or their distance away from the ship, our brains place them at equal distances apart along the curved "dome" overhead. But our straight line of sight makes them condense toward the horizon and acquire the appearance of a vertical stack at the edges.

Cockpit, Self-Draining Any boat meant to go to sea should be fitted with a self-draining cockpit and a bridge deck to prevent sea water from finding its way below.

Drain pipes should be large—at least 1¼ inches in diameter—because a cockpit takes a surprisingly long time to drain and the boat remains vulnerable to following seas until it has emptied.

Is there any disadvantage to, say, 3-inch drains? Well, yes. They would require 3-inch holes in the hull, which would make most sailors very uneasy.

If it's any comfort, in practice about half the contents of the cockpit will usually be spilled out fairly quickly as the boat rolls heavily in the kind of seas that would cause a pooping.

Color and Distance, Assistance in Judging In judging the distance of an object at sea, red colors generally appear closer than do blue colors.

In twilight, however, the effect is reversed. In this case, the human eye, as it becomes accustomed to growing darkness, is more sensitive to blue light than to red. As night falls, red objects grow correspondingly black.

Color Blindness, Frequency among Crew One in every 10 men is color blind.

Although color blindness is passed on from generation to generation by women, few of them suffer from it themselves. However, it would be wise to check for color blindness before entrusting a night watch to a crew member of either gender.

Colors, Unlucky Old superstition has it that it's presumptuous, and therefore unlucky, to paint a ship in the colors of the sea.

In olden times, vessels were seldom painted green or blue, since they had their own souls and could not presume to be part of the sea itself. Such presumption could be fatal.

See also: NAME, ATTRACTING BAD LUCK WITH

Companionway Ladder, Proportions of

Vertical ladders are almost unavoidable on small cruising sailboats, and the steps should be about 12 inches apart. A great luxury on a larger boat is to be able to descend sloping companionway steps with one's arms free to carry things. Sloping ladders must have their steps closer together, from 9 to 11 inches, and must have equal spacing of steps for safety reasons. The ladder can be as narrow as 15 inches in width, but 18 inches is more comfortable when sitting on the top step. But don't forget that sitting on the top step—and blocking everyone else's passage—is a crime of the highest order for all except the skipper and/or owner, who must be politely requested to move.

See also: APPENDIX: COMPANIONWAY STEPS, SPACING AND SLOPE

Compass, Angle of Dip Correction for Different Hemispheres

Some magnetic steering compasses and many magnetic hand-bearing compasses might need to be professionally adjusted if they're used in latitudes greater than 40 degrees in the hemisphere for which they are *not* compensated.

In the Northern Hemisphere, the north end of a compass needle tends to dip down toward the North Pole. The south end dips down toward the South Pole in the Southern Hemisphere. Some compasses are compensated for one hemisphere only, and will tilt the card until it drags against the edge of the bowl in the "wrong" hemisphere.

Where a card is free to tilt without experiencing drag—such as in a freely suspended bowl-type compass—the angle of dip is of less consequence until it becomes physically difficult to read the compass.

Compass, Testing

The fixed steering compass is the most important navigational instrument on a boat. It's a comparatively simple piece of equipment, but quality and accuracy can vary. On the whole, the old rule applies: You get what you pay for.

When buying a new magnetic compass, or checking one already installed, do two simple tests to give you a good idea of the instrument's quality:

- **Test for zero pivot friction.** Using a small magnet or piece of ferrous metal, deflect the compass about 5 degrees to one side, and then quickly remove the magnet or metal. The compass should return to its previous position exactly. Do a similar test from the other side.

- **Test for proper damping.** Deflect the compass card again, but this time let the card pivot through 30 degrees or so. When it returns, see how far it shoots past the original mark. A quality compass with proper damping has a minimum over-shoot and returns to its original position without excessive hunting backward and forward. A cheap compass that hunts endlessly will drive a helmsman to despair at night in a seaway.

Incidentally, don't for one moment imagine that you can cure bad deviation by installing a new compass. The new compass will have the same deviation as the old one, because deviation is caused by external factors on the boat around it.

Compass, Worst Enemies of Nothing destroys a compass more quickly than heat and strong, direct sunlight. When you're not using it, keep it shaded and cool by any means at your disposal.

Compass Card, Gradations of Compass cards for small boats don't need gradations marked in divisions of less than 5 degrees.

Experience has shown that it's very easy to estimate the positions of single degrees between two markers 5 degrees apart. Markings just 2 degrees apart, or individual degree markings, only tend to clutter the card, induce eye-strain, and confuse the watch on deck.

Compass Course, Result of Errors in
If your compass (or your calculations) should be out by 5 degrees, you will be one full mile off course for every 11.5 miles run.

Compass Light, Color of
There is only one color for a compass light: red. Even a dimly lit white light will destroy the helmsman's night vision.

Night vision is an asset little understood and little appreciated by people whose town lives are brightly lit wherever they find themselves at night. It's a wonderful gift from Nature, a manyfold heightening of visual acuity that vastly increases a person's ability to see in the dark. It can take 20 to 30 minutes to develop full night vision, and it's destroyed in a flash.

By lucky chance, red light has almost no effect on night vision. And if you wear red ski goggles for half an hour at your brightly lit supper table before going on night watch, you can emerge on deck fully night-adapted.

See also: LIGHTS, FAINT, LOCATING

Compass Light, Effect of Wiring
Direct current from the ship's batteries creates magnetic fields in wires supplying current to electrical items, including the compass light.

This magnetism in the wires can affect the accuracy of compasses. So the rule of thumb is to twist the two wires in the vicinity of the compass around each other in a loose spiral, by which means the individual magnetic effects are canceled out.

Coral Reefs, Navigating by Eye
The rule of thumb when navigating in areas strewn with uncharted coral reefs is to wait until the sun is high and behind you, from about 10 AM to 4 PM. Height above deck is an advantage to the spotter. Polarized

sunglasses can be helpful, but are not always an improvement. Calm, gray days make it very difficult to see far into the water.

Reading the water:

- Dark blue tones mean deep water, 20 fathoms or more.

- The blue becomes lighter with decreasing depth, and turquoise (vivid green-blue) is a warning of shoaling. It is the color of the coral sand covering a flat expanse of reef with 4 to 6 feet of water over it.

- Dark brown indicates coral heads.

- Brown or yellow indicates reefs with a depth of 3 or 4 feet over them.

- Green-brown means a grassy bottom.

- White means very shallow water.

Course Correction for Variation and Deviation

Without constant practice, it's difficult to remember how to apply compass deviation and variation. What remains in the mind is that east is least and west is best—but what does one do with that vague knowledge? One of the simplest and best ways to remember the rules is to apply the old mnemonic: Timid Virgins Make Dull Companions, Add Whisky.

In effect, this means writing on any blank space on your chart five headings marked T,V,M,D,C, and +W. They stand for True, Variation, Magnetic, Deviation, and Compass. The final column is simply a reminder that when you want to find any value in this chart, you must add westerly deviation and variation when moving from left to right (True to Compass). And, of course, you must subtract easterly deviation and variation.

If you move backward from right to left (Compass to True), you reverse the pluses and minuses. You subtract westerly deviation and variation and add easterly. Whether you move backward or forward depends on the values you already know. If you know any three, you can work out the other two. It's simple and about as foolproof as anything gets aboard a small boat. Write down all your courses, headings, and bearings. Every time. In full. All will become plain if you'll just write it down. And you'll be able to check later if you make a mistake.

Crew Overboard Routine

It's essential that you choose an emergency drill that you can follow automatically if a person falls overboard. It's not something you can leave until the last moment to look up in a reference book. You must choose a drill that suits your kind of boat, and you must practice it regularly.

The method you choose to recover a person overboard depends on the kind of boat and rescue gear you have. My personal preference on a sailboat is to change course to a broad reach immediately, from whatever course I'm sailing at the time, and then to come about and close-reach back to the person in the water. But there are other, equally effective methods. Find one that suits you and your boat.

On a powerboat, I would immediately turn 60 degrees to port or starboard, and then commence a handy turn that would take me straight back on a course reciprocal to the original.

However, even before maneuvering commences, there are certain vital actions to take:

- Throw overboard a cockpit cushion and/or lifebuoy attached to a dan buoy—a tall pole topped with a flag—to mark the position.

- Make a quick mental note of the compass course.

- Post a lookout whose job is to do nothing but keep an eye on the person in the water and to point toward him or her. If possible, the lookout should also start counting seconds aloud so the skipper can better judge the distance to return if the dan buoy is not visible.

Many experts assert that speed in turning—to keep the person overboard in sight—is the single most helpful procedure. Once the victim drifts out of sight, the chances of recovery are drastically reduced.

Recovering a person from the water is rarely easy, so practice your particular method whenever you can. And be careful. The law requires you to render aid—but you might incur liability if, through negligent or thoroughly incompetent action, you actually worsen the position of the person in the water.

The law seems to be harder on sailors than on landlubbers in this respect. Despite your best intentions as Good Samaritan, you must make your rescue effort in a manner compatible with the normal practice of good and safe seamanship, taking into account the prevailing circumstances of weather, traffic, and so on.

Obviously, your level of boating experience would be a factor in assessing liability. But if you should lose your head and back up to a person in the water, instead of approaching head-on as prudence dictates, you would almost certainly be liable if the victim were injured by the propellers.

Never forget that the most seamanlike thing to do might be to radio for help if another, more competent vessel were nearby and better able to effect rescue than you.

The more thought you give to crew overboard procedures, the more obvious it becomes that you should always have an acceptable plan worked out, that you should practice it from time to time, and that you should record the practice sessions in your ship's log.

C

41

Cruisers, Success Rate Among The success rate among people who set sail for a planned cruise of 6 to 18 months is 35 to 40 percent. Among those who declare they are "going off forever" or say their intention is to sail around the world, the rate drops to between 10 and 20 percent.

These figures were quoted by well-known authors Lin and Larry Pardey after they had been cruising for 14 years.

Their definition of success was: "Finding satisfaction or enjoyment from what you are doing; having a sense of harmony on board; feeling glad you had the experience; eager to continue or go off again."

Cruising, Cost of The French singlehander Bernard Moitessier coined a truism when he told a San Francisco audience that long-term cruising costs you "just as much as you have."

But here's a fascinating and more down-to-earth rule of thumb discovered by two of the world's most experienced voyagers, Lin and Larry Pardey:

Take your everyday, onshore living expenses. Subtract all of your automobile costs, two-thirds of your clothing expenses, your home rent or mortgage payments, and your mooring costs. Add one third to your food costs. The result is a close approximation of your cruising costs over an extended period.

Currents, Unreliable Never trust the charted set or rate of an ocean current near a coral reef, a jutting-out headland, or the steeply dropping edge of a continental shelf.

The speed and direction of currents can be changed drastically (usually speeded up) by local physical features such as these, and can vary from hour to hour with changes in tidal height and wind direction.

Currents, Wind-Driven A wind blowing steadily from one direction for 12 hours or more creates a surface current with a velocity of about 2 percent of the wind's average speed.

Interestingly, the current does not flow in the same direction as the wind. Because of the effect of the earth's rotation, the current is deflected to the right in the Northern Hemisphere and to the left in the Southern Hemisphere.

The amount of deflection varies with latitude, but ranges from about 15 degrees to as much as 45 degrees. The closer to the poles, the greater the deflection. The depth of the water also has an effect: the shallower the water, the greater the deflection.

C

43

Currents and Tidal Streams, Face-Saving Facts Some people can make you feel vastly inferior when they find out you don't know the difference between currents, tides, and tidal streams. The rules are simple, really: Current is a fairly steady and permanent *horizontal* movement of water, like a broad river running through the open ocean. A tidal stream also is a *horizontal* movement of water, but it varies frequently and regularly in speed and direction according to the state of the tide. Tide is the *vertical* movement of water.

Of course, you can't pile up water vertically, as a rising tide does, without its wanting to slide off sideways. This movement is called a tidal stream. It's not the tide that sets you on to the sandbank. It's the tidal stream. Remember that. It's vital to your social standing, in any later discussion of your mishap around the yacht club bar, that you should understand this.

One other thing: Streams and currents are identified by set and drift. The set is the direction they're moving toward (unlike wind, which is named for the direction it's coming from). And the drift is their speed over the ground in knots.

See also: TIDAL STREAMS (multiple entries)

D

Dangers, Keeping Clear of

The original "Rule of Thumb" was probably the principle adopted by shipmasters that they would never allow their vessels to approach a danger nearer than the distance that corresponded to a thumb's width on the chart in current use. Thus, they could navigate closer to dangers on a large-scale chart with plenty of detail than would be prudent on a small-scale chart with less. It's still a good principle.
—Geoff Lewis, *The Small-Boat Skipper's Handbook.*

Decks, Teak, Bare, Maintenance of

The maintenance of bare teak decks requires no expensive commercial preparations. Traditional maintenance on big ships was done by scrubbing the decks with blocks of soft sandstone the size of a Bible. At one time the British Royal Navy used fragments of sandstone from the ruined St. Nicholas Church in Great Yarmouth. They were known as holystones. In lieu thereof, you can use a plastic potscrubber and warm salt water with a dash of liquid detergent. However, if your seams are filled with the faint-hearted kind of compound that is harmed by detergent, use plain salt water.

Rub in a circular motion, or across the grain, to avoid scouring away the softer summer grain and making ridges. For this reason, do not, on any account, use a stiff-bristled brush.

Unlike oldtime sailors, for whom holystoning was a traditional Sunday chore, you need scrub your teak only once every month or two.

Your decks, however, should be damp with salt water at all times. It discourages rot, keeps the planking swollen, and prevents leaks. A weekly swish from a bucket is often enough; in the tropics, a daily washdown is not too frequent.

Decks, Teak, Bare, Removing Stains from

Drips of varnish should be wiped with thinner, left to dry, and then lightly sanded. Paint should be wiped away with thinners while still wet. Acetone should be used with caution because it dries out natural teak oils. Detergent, which does so to a lesser extent, usually removes the bulk of stains left by food and oils, leaving sun and salt water to finish the job. Rust stains and black marks can be removed with a 5-percent solution of oxalic acid. It's poisonous, so use it with caution and neutralize it well with salt water before sending it overboard.

D

45

Delivery Trips, Documentation for

A delivery skipper must carry a document proving he or she has the legal right to move the vessel.

It's normal for the legal owner to write a letter "to whom it may concern" stating the skipper's name, the extent of the delivery voyage (from which port to which), and the approximate duration of the voyage. The letter should say the skipper is empowered to act on the owner's behalf in all matters pertaining to the safety and operation of the vessel while engaged in its delivery.

The letter should be dated and legally notarized. It should be accompanied by photocopies, also notarized, of the ship's registration papers and any other documents applicable to the circumstances.

Depth Sounders, Choices

The depth sounder works by measuring how long it takes a sound to travel from the boat to the bottom of the sea and back again. As the speed of sound in water is known, the time the sound takes on its journey is proportional to the depth of the water. This is a very elementary calculation for modern electronic equipment.

The sound is emitted by the depth sounder's speaker, or transducer, at a frequency of between 50 and 200 kHz, which is too high for humans to hear. The rule is that the higher the frequency, within this range, the greater the detail the depth sounder produces, but at the cost of depth penetration. The lower the frequency, the greater the depth measurement, but at the cost of poorer resolution.

So sportfishers usually choose 200-kHz transducers for sharp pictures of the bottom and of fish, while serious navigators choose 50-kHz transducers to measure greater depths.

The accuracy of most units is plus or minus 5 percent.

Design, of New Yachts If most yachtsmen are conservative, then most designers set the example. It's a general rule of thumb that, in any new design, nine-tenths is 90 percent borrowed from existing plans and 10 percent adapted. Of the remaining tenth, 9 percent seems to fit into place by luck, 1 percent is genuine inspiration or "art," and 90 percent is pure trial and error.

Diesel Engines, Exhaust as a Trouble Indicator The exhaust gases from a diesel engine should normally be quite clear. Smoke of any color is an indication of trouble:

- *Black smoke* is the result of engine overload, a restricted air supply, or a malfunctioning fuel injector. Improperly burned particles of excess fuel are blown out of the exhaust.

- *Blue smoke* is formed by combustion of the engine's own lubricating oil. This can be the result of worn piston rings, valve guides, or oil seals. The oil can come from an overfilled air filter or an excess of oil in the crankcase.

- *White smoke* indicates either water vapor from dirty fuel (or a water leak into the cylinder) or atomized but completely unburned fuel. Air in the fuel can cause white smoke, too.

Diesel Engines, Fuel Problems The primary cause of failure, poor performance, and starting difficulty in a diesel engine is problems with the fuel.

Keeping small-boat fuel tanks entirely free of water, dirt, and bioorganisms is quite impossible. One does one's best, of course, but water will condense in the tank if it doesn't run in through the filler or breather pipes. Dirt particles find their way in with it, or form through chemical reaction in the tank. In addition, certain microscopic organisms in the vegetable kingdom thrive on a mixture of water and diesel fuel, forming a sludge that quickly blocks filters and stops the fuel from reaching the engine.

Biocidal additives greatly discourage their growth, after which the basic rule of thumb is to use filters to remove the water and dirt from the fuel. The importance of water separators and clean filters can hardly be exaggerated. Frequent inspection and changes of filters will do more than anything to stave off diesel engine failure.

And never let your tank run dry or turn the tank shutoff valve while the engine is running. If air is sucked into the system, or if it gets in while you're changing filters, you must go through the whole procedure of bleeding the fuel lines. If you don't know how to, you'd better learn, because unless your system is allegedly self-bleeding, the engine won't start with air in the lines no matter how long you press the starter button.

Diesel Fuel, Cetane Value of The cetane number of diesel fuel is an indication of how easily it ignites. The higher the number, the more readily it ignites.

A good grade of diesel fuel has a cetane rating of 50 and a sulphur content of less than 0.5 percent.

Dinghy, Hard, Capacity of A 7-foot hard
dinghy is generally reckoned to be the smallest that
can be used as a yacht's tender for two people.

If you have room to carry it, a bigger dinghy has
many advantages. A hard dinghy usually is easier
to row than is an inflatable, cheaper to operate with
an outboard engine, drier in a chop, and cheaper to
repair in the long run. But small cruisers may have
no option but to carry an inflatable.

Those with space for a hard dinghy, especially one
with a simple sailing rig, will surely find it makes
that 90 percent of cruising time not spent at sea *far*
more enjoyable.

Dinghy, Inflatable, Life of Liveaboard cruis-
ers on extended voyages usually find that an inflatable dinghy has a lifespan of three to four years.

Such dinghies are subjected to abnormal wear on
a year-round, day-in-day-out basis. Consequently,
long-term cruisers—those cruising for more than
two years—generally end up with a hard dinghy.
Sailors who use inflatables only during weekends
and annual vacations afloat should get 10 to 15
years of good service.

Direction, Measurement of Direction relat-
ing to small-craft navigation is measured to the
nearest whole degree on the 360-degree compass
rose. The motion of a small boat makes it pointless to
plot, or steer, a course or bearing to fractions of a
degree.

Displacement, Definition of To a naval archi-
tect, displacement is the total weight of a vessel and
her full crew, with all tanks two-thirds full and two-
thirds of the stores for which there is stowage space.
Because displacement literally equals the weight of
the water a boat displaces when she floats, it's also
a measure of a boat's underwater volume—the
amount from the waterline downward. Salt water,
for example, weighs 64 pounds per cubic foot, so the

underwater volume in cubic feet is displacement in pounds divided by 64. All too often, regrettably, displacement is incorrectly stated, for reasons varying from ignorance to deliberate deceit.

Displacement-to-Length Ratio This simple ratio gives you an idea of how "heavy" or "light" a boat is without being able to see her underwater body. It equals displacement in tons divided by 1/100 of the waterline in feet cubed.

D

49

Note that heavy displacement is no infallible indicator of strength or seakindliness, any more than light displacement is an indication of cramped accommodations or speed. However, generally speaking, spreading displacement over a longer waterline makes a boat faster and livelier.

Most cruisers are of medium to heavy displacement. Racing boats are usually light to ultralight. Of course, ideas about what constitutes light and heavy in a boat have changed over the years as new materials with improved strength-to-weight ratios have been pressed into use. These latest displacement-to-length ratios are regarded as conservatively reasonable:

380 to 1 or more:	Very heavy displacement
320 to 380:	Heavy
250 to 320:	Medium
120 to 250:	Light
50 to 120:	Very light
50 to1 or less:	Ultralight

Distance Off, Estimating by Eye In ordinarily clear weather, you can distinguish the shapes of prominent lighthouses, or houses and trees, from seaward at about 8 miles. The distance to the horizon is often surprisingly small, however. If your eye is 5 feet above water level, the horizon is only 2½ miles away. The old rule of thumb is that the distance of the horizon in miles is ⅞ of the square root of the height of the eye in feet.

Here are some other useful rules of thumb:

- A light-colored beach often is distinguishable at about 4 miles if you're standing on the deck of a typical small boat at sea.

- Individual windows in buildings are discernible by day or by night at 2 miles.

- A large buoy is visible at 2 miles.

- A small buoy is visible at 1½ miles, but color and shape are not discernible.

- The shape of a small buoy is discernible at 1 mile.

- The color of a large buoy is discernible at 1 mile.

- A person is distinguishable as a moving black dot without limbs at 1 mile.

- Movement of a person's legs or a rower's arms is discernible at 400 yards.

- Faces are discernible (but not recognizable) at 250 to 300 yards.

Distress Signals, Reliability of

Even if they're all within the expiration date, presume only 50 percent of your pyrotechnics will work properly.

This is a sensible rule for any small vessel venturing out of protected waters. The U.S. Coast Guard minimum requirements do not take into account the often damp and exposed stowage conditions of pyrotechnics on small yachts.

Dock Lines, Length of

The most useful and important of your dock lines are the springs, which prevent movement fore and aft in a berth. You should carry at least two springs that are a quarter longer than your boat is from stem to stern.

Many people scoff at the notion of carrying such long springs, but you'll never have cause to regret it. What's more, if you moor alongside in areas of large tidal range, you'll find your 125-percent springs absolutely invaluable for coping safely with drops in the water level. You'll be the one who's scoffing then. The longer the springs, the better your boat will maintain her position against a pier or wharf, and the less attention you'll need to give the lines as she rises and falls with the tide.

Dock Lines, Size of Splices The diameter of the eye splice in a dockline should be at least three times, and preferably four or five times, the diameter of the piling or bollard it fits over.

You might imagine from this that there is hardly anything too trivial or nautically esoteric to deserve its own rule of thumb. But, in fact, there's a good reason (as usual) for this ancient rule. A long eye splice is safer and lasts longer than a short one, because a short one tends to pull apart at the throat when tension is applied.

Dockage, Cost of As a general rule, dockage costs too much. In proportion to the value of his or her boat, the average boater pays more every year.

While slip fees tend to rise as the years roll by, the value of your boat goes down. Most people who leave their boats in the water year-round spend about 6 percent of their boat's value on marina fees every 12 months. So, in 15 years or less they will have spent as much on dockage as the boat is now worth.

Perhaps it's time slip fees were subsidized by the people who benefit from having a captive audience of boaters conveniently crammed into a space much smaller than they would occupy at moorings and far more easily accessible.

Who benefits from this? Utility companies, cable TV companies, marine mechanics, hull cleaners, detailers, boat cleaners, dockside hotels, stores, restaurants, and many others, including counties and states collecting sales and other taxes.

Many stores on land will refund your parking fee if you buy something from them. That's a principle boaters should start thinking about.

E

Ear Infections, from Sea Water One of the most common complaints among children living on cruising yachts, and adults who do a lot of skindiving in tropical waters, is ear infection. This can mostly be prevented by putting two drops of baby oil in each ear before diving to coat the sensitive skin of the eardrum. After the last swim of the day, rinse each ear with two or three drops of alcohol to kill bacteria. Better still, use 50-percent alcohol and 50-percent vinegar, because acidic vinegar lowers the pH value to a most unhealthy environment for bacteria. When spending all day in the water, repeat the treatment at noon. A note of caution, however: Be certain first that you have no leaks in your eardrums.

Echo Pilotage Note the time in seconds from the original signal to the return echo from a cliff, iceberg, wharf, or moored freighter. Every second's delay indicates a distance off of 1 cable, or 200 yards. Every 10 seconds' delay indicates a distance off of 1 mile.

This is one of those rules that could be useful in fog some day. A blank pistol shot produces a sharp echo, but the ship's bell or horn also suffices. Even a loud hail works at close quarters. The rule of thumb at work here is that sound travels about 1 mile in 5 seconds.

See also: SOUND, SPEED OF, IN WATER AND AIR

Electrical Bonding The rule of thumb is: All or nothing. Either link all metal parts of the hull and superstructure to a common ground or leave each to its own devices.

The aim of bonding is to even out differing electrical potentials that could cause stray currents and consequent corrosion. This is a controversial and complicated subject, though, and general solutions are inappropriate. It would be wise to study the subject and then make decisions on what to do.

Electrical Grounding The rule for boat DC systems is that the negative (−) wire runs to ground. If your electrical system was installed professionally, you can be pretty certain this is so. This means all protective fuses and/or circuit breakers must be in the positive (+) leads.

Electrical Wiring In general, electrical wiring for boats should have at least 20 strands in each wire to absorb flexing and vibration. The insulation should contain no paper or fabric.

Engine, Auxiliary, Size of Diesel engines have become smaller, lighter, and more powerful, so there's little excuse for an auxiliary sailboat to be underpowered these days. The old rule of thumb still holds good: The engine should be of such power that it can give a speed of at least 2 knots against a Force 5 wind with the weather shore as far as 2 miles distant.

Three to 4 horsepower per ton of displacement will do it, and a little more won't come amiss on occasion—not for extra speed, but to maintain a reasonable speed against strong winds and choppy seas.

A simple old formula for estimating the speed in knots that an auxiliary engine will give an average cruising yacht is to take the square root of the horsepower, multiply it by 15, and divide the answer by the beam of the boat in feet.

It's usually accurate to within half a knot; but apply the formula with some thought for displacement and wetted surface area. If the boat is of particularly heavy displacement or has more than normal wetted surface to cause drag, the actual speed will probably be lower. Light-displacement boats or centerboarders might well do better than the formula indicates.

Engine, Life Expectancy of

The average gasoline boat engine runs for 1,500 hours before needing a major overhaul. The average diesel engine runs for 5,000 hours under the same conditions—that is, more than three times as long.

Of course, these are very general rules of thumb, because the life of an engine depends on how it's used, abused, and maintained. These estimates, however, come from a man whose full-time job it has been for many years to persuade boaters to replace ailing used engines with new ones.

Cynically, therefore, we may assume that the figures concerning the life of the old engines are a little conservative. According to the same source, the typical gasoline boat engine gets a "good" 1,000 hours of operation. During the next 500 hours, minor troubles become increasingly likely, turning into major troubles as the 1,500-hour mark approaches.

It's interesting to note that an automobile engine runs an average of 2,900 hours—about double the running time of a gasoline boat engine—before requiring an overhaul at 100,000 miles. But most of the time, boat engines work harder than do car engines, and under worse conditions.

A well-maintained gasoline boat engine run under the best conditions might well run for more than 1,500 hours without a major overhaul; but many that operate under the most atrocious conditions of salt air, damp bilges, intermittent operation, and pure neglect certainly get fewer hours.

Diesel engines are built more heavily, and to finer tolerances, than are gasoline engines. They thus accept much more abuse and often deliver 8,000 hours of hard work before requiring major surgery. At this rate, in theory, a well-maintained diesel auxiliary might well last the life of the boat. After all, the average boat owner logs 200 engine hours a year, so it would take 40 years to do 8,000 hours.

Unfortunately, in practice things are rather different. Engines like to run long and steadily. The shorter the running time between stops, and the longer the idle time between runs, the fewer the hours they deliver before needing to be carted off to the engine hospital.

E

55

Engine Conditions, Ideal It's an unfortunate fact that most boat engines (and above all those in auxiliary sailboats) work under adverse conditions. What they really need is rarely what they actually get. Naval architect and author Dave Gerr says engine compartments should be supplied with oodles of dry, cool (50 degrees F), clean air. The very minimum fresh air vent area (in square inches) for natural ventilation without blowers is found by dividing engine horsepower by 3.3, says Gerr.

Incidentally, two of the most important rules of thumb for engine compartment blowers on gasoline engines are that they should always be set to exhaust, not to blow air in, and that they should be run for a *minimum* of 5 minutes before starting the engine.

Engine Mounts, Size of Poorly mounted engines can cause excessive vibration and result in expensive damage to the drivetrain. Properly mounted engines are fitted to two heavy steel or aluminum angles that run the full length of the engine, and which are through-bolted to the engine beds or stringers. The rule of thumb is to attach each angle to the stringer with four bolts. The minimum diameter of each bolt in inches can be found by dividing engine weight in pounds by 4,000—but in no case should the bolts be less than ⅜-inch diameter. The engine mounts should be bolted to the angle.

Engine Oil, When to Check
You simply cannot check the level of the oil in your engine too often.

You should check it at least once a day and preferably before every start. Weekend boaters checking the oil before starting up should be very suspicious of levels that are too high or too low.

Too high a level might be a clue that water has found its way into the oil sump. You could crack the cylinder head, break a piston, or both, just by trying to turn the engine over.

Too low a level could indicate an oil leak that could lead to engine seizure.

Whenever there is a large deviation from normal, regard it as an urgent warning. Start looking for more clues or seek expert help.

Exhaust Line, Pitch of
Engine exhaust piping or tubing should be installed with a continuous drop to the exit of at least 1 inch for every 2 feet of run.

There should be no possibility of sea water or engine cooling water finding its way back up the pipe to the exhaust manifold, thence to the cylinders and pistons.

Engines set so low in the boat that their exhaust manifolds are at or below water level need exhaust risers to gain the initial height needed. In wet exhausts, cooling water enters the riser in the downward leg.

F

Fathom, Derivation of In many languages, the word *fathom* was derived from a word meaning two arms' width, or an embrace, which itself is derived from the Latin root for *arms*. In the Mediterranean languages, the word for fathom still makes its derivation clear: in Portuguese it's *braça*; in Spanish, *braza*; in Italian, *braccio*. Our word fathom comes from the Old English *fæthm*, which meant *the outstretched arms*.

The lead-line used to measure the depth of water was measured between outstretched arms. Different sailors had different-sized embraces, of course, so the unit known as the fathom was eventually standardized at six feet—which is actually quite an enthusiastic embrace.

The fathom is such a useful natural measure that one can only express astonishment that it's being ousted by that most unnatural metric measure, the meter. At six feet, the fathom is a subdivision of a cable, which is 100 fathoms (600 feet). The cable, in turn, is a subdivision of the nautical mile, which, for practical purposes, is taken to be 6,000 feet (or 10 cables).

Fear, Experience of At sea, it's better to feel fear early than late.

Seasoned sailors are subject to anxiety before danger arrives. By anticipating it, they are better placed to meet it or even avoid it. Inexperienced sailors may wander blindly into danger and then become paralyzed with fear when it's too late.

Fear, Widespread, Occurrence of Fear

seems to be a natural part of boating, especially among singlehanded voyagers. According to research by solo sailor Dr. David Lewis, in collaboration with the Medical Research Council in Great Britain, four out of five contestants in the 1960 singlehanded transatlantic race experienced "acute fear."

In general, there were two types: generalized initial tensions and anxieties lasting a few days, and then more specific apprehension caused by potential danger, such as an approaching storm or the proximity of hazards.

Interestingly, Dr. Lewis found that often the extent of fear was not recalled after the fact. He concluded: "Observations noted *at the time* are the only valid ones."

Fiberglass, Drawbacks of Despite its over-

whelming popularity as a boatbuilding material, glass fiber-reinforced plastic has some major drawbacks.

Apart from its lack of aesthetic appeal, fiberglass has one of the lowest stiffness-to-weight ratios of any boatbuilding material. It weighs about 94 pounds per cubic foot, while considerably stiffer mahogany weighs 35 pounds per cubic foot. Designers and builders try to keep hull and deck weight down by reducing the thickness of fiberglass, but this all too often results in floppy sections that "oil-can," or give way disconcertingly when you walk on them.

Fiberglass, Sandwich Construction Foam

sandwich or balsa-cored hulls and decks are thicker than solid fiberglass, but about eight times stiffer for the same total amount of fiberglass. They thus need less internal stiffening. The dimensions of a composite sandwich should be roughly as follows:

Core: 2.2 times the thickness of the equivalent solid fiberglass skin

Inner fiberglass skin: 0.3 times the single-skin thickness

Outer fiberglass skin: 0.4 times the single-skin thickness

Fiberglass, Standard Laminate
The great majority of fiberglass boats use the same laminate—alternating layers of 1½-ounces-per-square-yard chopped strand mat and 24-ounces-per-square-yard woven roving, wetted out with standard polyester resin.

These two layers constitute one *ply*, and each ply is about ³⁄₃₂ inch thick. Such a laminate weighs about 94 pounds per cubic foot, of which weight about 35 percent is in the glass fibers. In normal boatbuilding, the extra strength of epoxy resin is rarely justified when compared with the extra cost.

Fiberglass, Stiffening of Hulls
To provide the necessary stiffness a vessel requires, most solid fiberglass hulls need five or more longitudinal stringers evenly spaced on each side of the inside of the hull, and at least five structural bulkheads roughly evenly spaced along the length.

Fiberglass, Thickness of Solid Hulls
Skin thickness in inches should equal at least 0.07 plus the waterline length in feet divided by 150.

Thickness usually varies from topsides down, with about 15 percent less than the average hull thickness in the upper topsides, and about 15 percent more than the average thickness at and below the waterline.

Powerboats should increase thickness by about 1 percent for every knot of boat speed over 10 knots.

Fiddles, Height of
The old rule of thumb was that a yacht's saloon table should be fitted with fiddles 1½ inches high. Such fiddles, correctly spaced according to the size of plates, will keep a meal securely in place at quite a steep angle of heel.

Fiddles should fold down or be removable to allow the table to be used for other work, especially in port.

Figureheads, Derivation of
Figureheads represent a sacrifice to the ancient gods of the wind and the sea. They should always be representations of human beings, never creatures of the sea.

In the beginning, real human heads were placed on the bowsprit of a vessel starting her first voyage, and more often than not the heads were of beautiful maidens—hence, perhaps, the term *maiden voyage*. This great sacrifice was intended to ensure the safe passage of the vessel and her crew across the stormy waters ruled by Neptune, Aeolus, and a host of minor deities. It was also supposed to provide the ship with a soul, since every ship needs a soul. The belief was that when the head fell off the bowsprit, it was a sign that the gods had accepted the sacrifice and that the young woman's soul had entered the ship.

Today, of course, in the age of female emancipation, mariners no longer dare use live maidens for figureheads, which may explain the glut of soulless, plastic, look-alike vessels that fill our marinas today.

Fire, Most Common Locations of
Most fires or explosions on boats occur in the engine room or galley.

Cooking gas or gasoline mixed with air forms very powerful explosive combinations. A half-teacup of gasoline, mixed with about 15 times that volume of air, has sufficient energy stored in it to destroy a large yacht.

Fire, Extinguishing
Three basic ways to extinguish a fire are:

- Starve it of oxygen.
- Remove the material it is feeding on.
- Cool the burning material below the combustion point.

Water is best for paper, wood, most materials, and alcohol. Oil, gasoline, kerosene, diesel, and cooking fats need a dry powder, foam, or chemical gas extinguisher. Fires involving high-voltage electricity must not be fought with water. If you have only water, cut off the electricity first. As a general rule, always aim at the base of the fire, the point at which flames originate. It also makes sense to keep extinguishers near, but not exactly at, points where fire is most likely to break out.

Fire Extinguishers, Discharge Time Most fire extinguishers found aboard small pleasure vessels have a discharge time of between 8 and 20 seconds. This is a very good reason for using them effectively from the very start. The three basic rules for using extinguishers are: Don't delay, get close, and aim low.

Fire Extinguishers, Location of It sounds elementary, but a marine surveyor tells me he sees it all the time: Don't place your extinguishers right where a fire is likely to break out. Place them *nearby*, on your escape routes. Usually there should be at least one near the galley stove, and another near the engine. An extra one on a bulkhead up forward and one available from the cockpit are good ideas, too. Fire at sea is a fearsome thing, particularly in a fiberglass hull.

First Aid When giving first aid, the most basic rule of thumb is: Don't panic. Make haste slowly.

There are only three situations that call for really fast action: Starting breathing, stopping bleeding, and dealing with snakebite. Fortunately, snakes are rare on yachts. And if you don't know how to get a victim breathing again, or staunch the flow of blood, now's the time to start thinking about a first-aid course.

With all other sicknesses and accidents, you'll

likely have more time than medical knowledge at your disposal, so make a note of Rule Number Two: Always take first aid to the victim, not vice-versa.

Make the patient as comfortable as possible and don't move him or her any more than necessary to get away from hazards, including being swept overboard. Then get on the radio, read your Ship Captain's Medical Guide or, after unhurried contemplation, take such action as ordinary common sense dictates.

Fishing, Definition of

A sailing vessel is obliged by law to keep clear of "a vessel engaged in fishing."

But that doesn't mean she has to give way to any Tom, Dick, or Harry with a fishing pole hanging over the stern. Both national and international navigation rules define "a vessel engaged in fishing" as "any vessel fishing with nets, line trawls or other fishing apparatus which restrict maneuverability."

The rules specifically *exclude* "a vessel fishing with trolling lines or other fishing apparatus which does not restrict maneuverability." So the rule of thumb is that "a vessel engaged in fishing," in terms of the collision regulations, is one that is unable to maneuver to keep clear of anyone else.

Incidentally, beware of the glib misconception that a sailing boat must always give way to a fishing boat. That's not so—unless the fishing boat happens to be "engaged in fishing" at the time.

Flags, Dimensions of

Ensigns: 1 inch on the fly for every foot of boat length overall. The hoist should be about two-thirds of the fly. The staff should be about twice the length of the hoist.

Courtesy flags: About ⅝ inch on the fly for each foot of boat length.

Flags, Positions of

Club burgee: Worn at the masthead or from the starboard spreader beneath the courtesy flag. One burgee at a time only, please.

Fun flags: Worn at the port spreader

Racing yacht battle flags: Worn halfway up the forestay

Racing yacht class pennants: Worn at the backstay

Old Glory: Worn at the stern staff; or from a position two-thirds of the way up the mainsail leech; or from the afterpeak of a gaff-rigged vessel while underway.

Notes:

- When racing, the ensign is not flown.

- When outside U.S. territorial waters, only the Stars and Stripes (not the U.S. Yacht Ensign) may be flown.

- If the burgee features a five-pointed star, the flag must be flown with the point of the star upwards. The usual penalty for transgression is drinks all round.

- A cocktail party flag flown upside down usually means bring your own drinks. Of course, it could also indicate that the flag was raised by a host already in the party mood.

- Flags are *worn* by a yacht; they are *flown* by the owner.

Flags, Times to Hoist and Lower The
ensign is hoisted at 0800 hours and lowered at sundown. However, it may be hoisted prior to 0800 if leaving port earlier, provided there is adequate daylight for visibility.

The burgee is hoisted and lowered at the same times as the national ensign, but the burgee

F

63

should be flown only while the owner is aboard.

To sum up: Fun flags, battle flags, class pennants, and informative flags may be worn at the stays and the port spreader. The starboard spreader is reserved for a national courtesy flag and one burgee. The ensign positions are sacrosanct. In emergencies, however, an ensign could be flown from the backstay.

Flotation, Requirements for Ballasted Hulls
After it has been holed, keeping afloat a vessel with a fiberglass hull having up to 35 percent lead ballast requires a minimum of 1 pound of added buoyancy for every 1.6 pounds of displacement. An additional safety margin of 25 percent is recommended. Wooden hulls should add buoyancy equivalent to the weight of the ballast and engine, plus 25 percent.

This is an average rule of thumb, and different boats might need more or less flotation. The fastening and positioning of flotation material are important. If in doubt, check with a marine engineer or naval architect. Air bags offer about 63 pounds of lift per cubic foot. Foam provides a lift of about 62 pounds per cubic foot.

See also: APPENDIX: WEIGHTS OF SOME COMMON MATERIALS FOUND IN BOATS

Flotsam and Jetsam, Definitions of
These words are often wrongly regarded as interchangeable. In fact, flotsam is all that remains floating on the surface of the water after a vessel has accidentally sunk. Jetsam, on the other hand, is cargo or gear that has deliberately been thrown overboard to help save a vessel in heavy seas or other threatening circumstances.

There seems to be no requirement, incidentally, that to be known as such, jetsam should float. Presumably, if such action is to no avail, and the vessel later sinks, the jetsam (at least, that portion of it that does float) might suddenly become flotsam.

But this is not certain. Of course, if you attached a buoy to your jetsam, it might better be described as lagan. But only a sea lawyer would know for sure. Or care.

Fog, Action to Take in If you see fog approaching, fix your position, or at least take a bearing. If possible, find water too shallow for large ships and anchor there. Remember to ring your bell for about five seconds every 60 seconds, and keep a sharp listening watch. If, while at anchor, you hear a vessel approaching, sound one short blast, one prolonged, and one short (Morse code "R") to warn her of your presence. If under power, sound the appropriate signal and stop the engine every few minutes and listen for other vessels.

See also: APPENDIX: SOUND SIGNALS, MOST COMMON

Fog, Different Types of It's probably of scant consolation to any boater caught in fog to be informed that fog is usually formed in one of four ways. However, those mariners whose thirst for knowledge exceeds their fear of being run down by a steamer might wish to take the time to learn the correct name for the fog they are cursing:

Radiation fog forms in near-calms on clear nights, when the ground radiates its heat into space and cools down.

Advection fog forms when warm, moist air from any source flows over a colder sea or lake.

Steam fog, or sea smoke, occurs when cold air flows across much warmer water.

Precipitation fog forms when warm rain falls through a surface layer of cold air.

Fog, Distribution of In U.S. waters, the frequency of fog diminishes as one moves from north to south. But the tailoff is quicker on the Atlantic coast than on the Pacific coast.

Southern California, from Los Angeles to San

Diego, has about three times the fog found at the same latitudes on the Atlantic coast. On the West Coast, the foggiest stretch (10 percent of the time) is from the Strait of San Juan de Fuca to Point Arguello, California. On the East Coast, there is a similar incidence of fog from the Bay of Fundy to Montauk Point, New York. The foggiest of the foggy? The coast of Northern California and the coast of Maine—about 20 percent of the year.

Fog, How Noises Differ in
In fog, distant noises mostly sound low and dull. Nearer noises are higher and brighter.

Over long distances through air, high frequencies are filtered out of the sound spectrum. For instance, nearby thunder crackles and crashes. Faraway thunder rumbles and rolls. The same principle applies to ships' horns and other warning signals. A loud, high-pitched whistle could mean imminent collision. Fog also carries sound much more efficiently than does dry air. Even the faintest noises are carried long distances, which makes distance judging even more difficult.

Fog, Prediction of
The basic rules about fog are simple. Warm air can hold more moisture than can cold air. Thus, if warm air saturated with moisture is chilled, the moisture will condense out and fog will result.

While the principle is simple, the actual art of predicting when fog will occur is rather more complicated. What you need to know is what percentage of moisture the air contains, and therefore what temperature it needs to be brought down to before condensation occurs. This temperature is known as the *dew point*.

To find out how much moisture there is in the air around you, you need either a hygrometer with wet-bulb and dry-bulb readings, or a fascinating instrument called a psychrometer, which is basically the same thing as a hygrometer but faster acting because you whirl it around your head on the end of a lanyard. Once you know how wet or dry the air is, you can find the dew point from tables.

Some people can judge when fog is coming by watching the way their breath condenses or by feeling the way their bones ache. Some can tell by the noise distant sounds make. The wise skipper simply presumes fog can happen at any time and plans all navigation accordingly.

Fog, Size Distortion in With visibility in fog between approximately 30 and 150 yards, vessels and other objects appear twice as large as normal.

This illusion also effectively doubles their speed of approach and instills great fear in the hearts of mariners.

Fog, Steering a Straight Course Without a Compass To steer a straight course, stream aft a drogue of any kind attached by a light line or fishing nylon. Attach the forward end high in the bow, or to the mast, and keep the line centered where it passes over the stern.

The longer your line, the straighter your course will be, but this method is strictly for short distances only, possibly as far as a mile in the right circumstances. Make sure the line is correctly centered. If it's not, you'll go around in a circle.

Foresail Sheets, Fouling of Foresail sheets have an infuriating habit of snagging themselves on deckware or mast cleats while the boat is in the process of going about. An ancient wrinkle that keeps blood pressure at a safe level in the cockpit is to bend a line to the mast at gooseneck level or a little above and to make the other end fast, after tautening, to the stemhead or samson post.

Foresails, Headsails, and Jibs It would take a brave individual to lay down the law about which is which these days. In common usage, they're inter-changeable, and any attempt to define them more narrowly is usually regarded as pedantic.

However, the threat of being dubbed a pedant has never particularly bothered me, so let's take a closer look at rules of thumb that may have been forgotten in the rush of modern times.

In most fore-and-aft-rigged sailing yachts, a forestaysail is a sail set on the forestay, which extends from the stemhead to a point at or near the top of the mast. This word is usually (and confus-ingly) abbreviated to *foresail*. It can vary in size and shape from a large low-cut Genoa, to a medium-sized high-cut Yankee, to a tiny storm staysail.

(Of course, in a schooner the foresail is the sail that extends aft from the foremast, so the sails in front of it are called jibs—starting from forward, the flying jib, the inner jib, and the staysail or jumbo jib. Frankly, this is a confounded nuisance to anyone try-ing to simplify the headsail mess, and my advice is to ignore schooners completely unless you are forced to sail on one or talk about them.)

A *headsail* is any sail set forward of the foremast, or mainmast if you have only one mast. It's a generic term for foresails, jibs, and even squaresails, spin-nakers, gennakers, bloopers, and the like, although the usage usually is restricted to foresails and jibs.

A *jib* is (pedantically) a foresail set forward of the forestay, whether hanked to a topmast stay of its own or, more properly, set flying from its halyard. The jib is sometimes defined as the foremost head-sail.

What this boils down to in most cases is that headsails are any sails set ahead of the mainmast. Foresails are hanked or rolled on to the forestay, the one that ends at the stem head. Jibs are sails set for-ward of the forestay.

But I doubt that there will ever be any general

agreement on this. It's not the sort of subject that rivets a modern sailor's attention and compels him or her to action. Thus, my guess is that we are doomed to wallow in a sloppy sea of indifference and imprecise usage until sails are superseded by solar power or miniature atomic reactors.

My reference sources are *Chapman's Piloting, Seamanship & Small Boat Handling*, *Encyclopedia of Nautical Knowledge* by McEwen and Lewis, and *Cruising Under Sail* by Eric Hiscock.

Freeboard in Sailboats, Classic Proportions of

The average height of freeboard in a classic cruising sailboat is 2⅓ inches per foot of beam. Freeboard is regarded as one of the most important features contributing to safety, because high freeboard provides a greater range of stability. On the other hand, too much freeboard adversely affects sailing ability, particularly to windward.

Friday, Sailing on

It is widely believed throughout the world that to sail on a Friday is to invite disaster.

This old rule may have originated with the crucifixion of Christ, which occurred on a Friday, but the belief is common among sailors of other religions as well.

Yet we know full well that countless vessels set sail every Friday and complete their passages safely. How can this be? It simply means that their skippers have earned enough points in their Black Boxes to overcome the bad luck of sailing on Friday.

If you have a choice, do not sail on a Friday. If you are forced to, then be very sure your Black Box is crammed full.

See also: BLACK BOX THEORY, VIGOR'S

Fuel, Recommended Tankage

The amount of fuel carried depends mostly on the design of the boat and the use to which it is put.

For instance, a 50-gallon tank of diesel feeding a 25-h.p. auxiliary cruising at 80 percent of top speed is sufficient to propel a 33-foot sailboat 300 miles at 7 knots in calm weather.

That same amount of fuel would take a twin-engined 40-foot sportfisher only about 33 miles at 40 knots. This boat would need 450 gallons to cover 300 miles at that speed.

Planing hulls need far more power than do displacement hulls, and thus use more fuel per mile. But their capacity to carry fuel is limited because their planing ability is affected by weight.

So naval architects build in as little tankage as seems appropriate, taking into account the nature of the boat, reasonable usage, and the distance between refueling stops in its normal area of operations.

Fuel, Weight of Gasoline weighs about 6.1 pounds per gallon. Diesel weighs about 7.1 pounds per gallon. By and large, both gasoline and diesel engines use about 0.6 pound of fuel per horsepower per hour. On average, diesel fuel contains about 140,000 BTUs per gallon, or 10 percent more energy than the same volume of gasoline.

Fuel, Where It Goes This is how your engine uses the energy you paid for:

- 35 percent in heat given up to the atmosphere
- 25 percent in heat and vibration absorbed by surrounding water
- 10 percent to overcome wave resistance
- 6 percent to overcome wave formation and prop wash against the hull
- 7 percent to overcome skin friction

- 2 percent wasted in friction at the propeller shaft

- 1 percent to overcome air resistance

This leaves about 13 to 14 percent of the original energy to turn the propeller.

Fuel Consumption, Diesel A diesel engine consumes about 1 gallon per hour for every 18 h.p. *used*. Alternatively, you can determine the number of gallons consumed per hour by multiplying horsepower used by 0.055.

Note: An engine at cruising speed usually uses about two-thirds of its maximum available horsepower. Most marine engines are designed to run continuously at between 60 and 75 percent of maximum speed, with diesels tending more toward the top of the range.

Fuel Consumption, Gasoline Four-stroke inboard engines need about 1 gallon per hour for every 10 h.p. used. Alternatively, the number of gallons consumed per hour can be found by multiplying horsepower used by 0.100 (see note above). Outboards might use considerably more, with two-cycle motors showing greater thirst than do four-cycle motors.

Fuel Economy Any attempt to force a displacement yacht beyond its maximum theoretical hull speed brings vast penalties in fuel consumption for minimal gains in velocity. Conversely, slowing down a little almost always is rewarded by disproportionate gains in economy, thus range. This principle applies to high-speed planing hulls also—but only up to the point at which they start to drop off the plane, after which they tend to lose efficiency.

See also: SPEED, MAXIMUM (multiple entries)

Fuel Reserves If you're planning to power to a destination where there's no chance of refueling, the old rule of thumb is to earmark one-third of your fuel to get there and one third to get back. The other third is your emergency reserve.

Fuel Tanks, Shape of Tanks should be deep and narrow to aid in stability when rolling. The long dimension should be fitted along the fore-and-aft line of the boat.

G

Gaff Mainsail, Proportions of Gaff mainsails are about as rare as hen's teeth these days, but lest we forget, here are some traditional rules for their proportions:

Luff: Between ⅔ and ⅘ of the foot.

Head: Between ⅗ and ⅔ of the foot.

Gaff: About 35 degrees from vertical, except that a gaff on a tall, narrow sail needs to be more horizontal, otherwise it sags to leeward; hence the shape of a schooner's foresail. The springstay also prevents a schooner's foresail from being shaped with a high peak.

Boom angle: The height of the mainsail clew above water level should be 1.4 times the height of the tack above water level.

Gales, Frequency of The frequency of gales obviously varies with location and season. But round-the-world yachts making the popular westward circumnavigations through the trade-wind belts in the most favorable seasons, and rounding the Cape of Good Hope, report an average of two sailing days per 100 in ocean gales of Force 8 (34 knots) or higher.

Galley, Placement of Traditionally, a sailboat's galley is placed on the port side.

It's easier and safer to cook when the galley is down to leeward, and the port side is the leeward side when the boat is on the starboard tack. Now the boat won't have to go about to avoid another vessel when she's hove-to on the starboard tack, because she'll have the right of way. This means the cook won't be disturbed by the necessity to go about. And that's important. Sea cooks can be very temperamental about these things.

Galley Stove, How to Gimbal The axis of the gimbals for the galley stove should run fore and aft.

Unlike a compass, the stove is usually gimbaled in one plane only. If you install the stove athwartships, and gimbal it with the axis running from port to starboard, it will tilt as the boat heels and be completely unworkable. It's possible that you could get away with it on a multihull, of course, but it would be wiser not to tempt fate.

The second rule is that the pivots for the swinging galley stove should be level with the hot-plate, so the motion resembles that of a see-saw. If the pivot point is higher than the hot plate (as is sometimes seen) the stove will swing like a pendulum and spill the contents of pots through centrifugal force.

Incidentally, until you've worked with one you might not realize why, but the opening to the firebox of a solid-fuel stove should face fore-and-aft, not athwartships.

Global Positioning System (GPS), Limitations of Latitude and longitude plotted on paper charts from a GPS readout can be a mile or more in error because of the differing survey base references used over the centuries.

Like Loran, a GPS returns very accurately to a waypoint position it has been to before. But it should not be relied upon to enter a strange harbor in poor visibility or to keep you clear of a low-lying coral reef. For safety, use GPS to identify a landfall, and then use compass bearings to plot your position on the chart and proceed with pilotage as usual.

As a general rule, it would be extremely foolhardy to rely *solely* on a GPS receiver for coastal navigation and pilotage. A working knowledge of ordinary coastal navigation, celestial navigation, or both, also is essential. A cruising skipper who depends on GPS alone is, in the words of Lin and Larry Pardey, endangering the lives of his or her crew by placing them "only a diode away from disaster."

Differential GPS sets receive a correction broadcast by a ground-based radio station to eliminate the error and make the displayed latitude and longitude agree with the local charted coordinates.

Green Flash, at Sunset
On rare occasions, when atmospheric conditions are right, you might see a green flash in the very last rays of the setting sun as it sinks into the sea.

It has been mentioned by several well-known ocean voyagers, including Eric Hiscock, and I have seen it in the mid-South Atlantic on a calm evening in the southeast trades. It lasts only a fraction of a second, but you can prolong it slightly by standing up as it occurs. If you're really lucky, your boat will be lifted on a swell at exactly the right moment. But don't count on it.

G

75

Griping, Causes of
Griping is an old term for the tendency of a hull to turn into the wind. Griping is countered by weather helm. A wide hull with a broad transom and hard bilges frequently gripes in a puff. A tall rig gripes more readily than does a low one because its center of effort moves farther out from the centerline as it heels, and so gains more leverage.

Thus, in (greatly simplified) theory, the best mannered boat would be a narrow-beamed double-ender under a low rig. She should have similar areas immersed fore and aft when heeling or rolling so that the hull doesn't alter its longitudinal trim. In practice, luckily, almost all modern cruising boats designed without regard to racing rules are reasonably docile when heeled.

Conversely, boats built to racing rules such as the

International Offshore Rule (I.O.R.) frequently carry their excessive beam a long way aft to gain sail-carrying ability and speed off the wind. Such boats are, as a rule, unbalanced. As they heel, the stern lifts and the bow sinks. The effect is to induce griping that is often powerful enough to overwhelm the rudder, which loses potency as it is lifted out of the water with heeling. Beware. Such boats are inherently unseaworthy. Many do make long passages with large, fit, and expert crews, but in such cases expertise and experience form a substitute for inherent seaworthiness.

Unfortunately, many modern boats sold as coastal cruisers are built to designs influenced by the I.O.R. and other rules. The style, glamour, and perceived performance (a myth) that rubs off from racers ensures that these pseudo-cruisers sell in quantity as production boats. What the brochures don't say is that these characteristics sometimes come at the cost of ultimate seaworthiness.

See also: BALANCED HELM, FACTORS AFFECTING MONOHULL SAILBOATS; AND WEATHER HELM, BENEFITS OF

H

Hallucinations, Occurrence of Hallucinations caused by fatigue are frequent among sailors undertaking long voyages. Psychologist Dr. Gilin Bennet reported that 50 percent of the competitors in the 1972 singlehanded race across the North Atlantic experienced one or more illusions or hallucinations.

Probably the most famous victim was Joshua Slocum, who described how the imaginary pilot of the *Pinta* took care of the *Spray* when he was ill.

Most hallucinations are imaginary perceptions or sensations of hearing voices or seeing scenes that do not actually exist.

Research indicates that dreams are important for mental health. People denied dreams through lack of sleep are subject to an alternative in the form of hallucinations, a sort of parade of waking dreams.

Thus, the rule of thumb is not to be unduly frightened by hallucinations, which are primarily a result of sleep deprivation, aided in some cases by monotony and solitude. They can be avoided by getting plenty of sleep, eating interesting meals, keeping mentally active, and trying to vary the day's activities.

See also: VOICES, ILLLUSION OF HEARING

Halyards, Types of Halyards can be all wire, all rope, or a mixture of both. Halyard stretch is avoided on most modern sailing yachts by having 7 x 19 stainless steel wire halyards with rope tails. The rule of thumb is that when the sail is raised, the wire should end a few inches before the halyard winch.

This means the barrel of the winch accommodates rope, not wire, and can be cleated off nearby. The small length of rope between the winch and the start of the wire won't stretch significantly. Incidentally, contrary to what many people assume, the wire-to-rope splice is designed to take the full strain applied to the halyard. It will, in any case, when the sail is reefed.

All-wire halyards need special reel winches that never seem quite at home on a small boat. Easing the considerable strain on thin wire is far more nerve-racking than dealing with soft rope.

All-rope halyards are perfectly acceptable for cruising yachts and small daysailers—in fact, any sailing yacht other than the out-and-out racer. Pre-stretched, double-braided Dacron stretches very little underway, and is easily taken up with a turn or two on the winch. Nice fat oversized rope halyards stretch even less, and there's no windage penalty if they run down inside the mast.

See also: APPENDIX: HALYARD SIZES FOR AVERAGE APPLICATIONS

Hatches, Dimensions of

Most sailors get on well with a hatch opening 24 inches by 24 inches, but a few inches more in either direction would not go amiss. The absolute minimum clearance space in an access hatch is 22 inches square.

Naval architect and author Dave Gerr offers the following rule of thumb for the minimum size of hatch (in square feet) needed to pass a sail through:

Racing boats: Sail area in square feet divided by 160

Cruising boats: Sail area in square feet divided by 200

Headroom, Definitions of

The generally accepted definition of the term *full standing head-*

room is 6 feet 1 inch clear under the deck beams or headliner. Clear sitting headroom of 4 feet 0 inches to 4 feet 9 inches is adequate and practical for small boats. Anything more—until full standing headroom is reached—is merely an irritating continual invitation to stand and hit one's head.

Height of Eye, for Sextant Navigation
The usual correction for the height of eye above water level in small boats is minus three minutes (– 3').

The calculated altitude worked out from the tables presumes your sextant is at sea level, so a correction must be made to all sights except those taken with a bubble sextant or an artificial horizon. The correction of – 3' equates to an actual height above water of about 8 feet.

Hobbyhorsing, Causes of
A sailboat that hobbyhorses excessively—that is, rears and plunges seemingly in the same spot in the sea—will be exceedingly slow to windward and irritate her crew excessively.

In the absence of any major design fault, hobbyhorsing is caused by too much weight in the bows and the stern, but particularly in the bows, where heavy ground tackle and chain often accumulate. Weight aloft also contributes to the moment of inertia, which is a prime cause of hobbyhorsing.

When the ends are lightened by moving heavy weights to the center of the boat, and excessive weight is removed from the mast, the difference in performance is often remarkable and much appreciated by crews.

Hooks, Shackles, and Rings, Strength of
A hook is likely to be the weakest part of any fitting. The old rule of thumb to find the working load of a hook in tons is diameter squared divided by 2, where diameter is the diameter in inches of the metal at the back of the hook.

For other fittings, the working load is roughly as follows:

D shackle: Diameter squared times 3

Bow shackle: Diameter squared times 2½

Ring bolt: Diameter squared times 2

Eye bolt: Diameter squared times 5

Horsepower, Generated by Humans

It is fairly well established in sports medicine that the average man in good condition can produce about ¼ h.p. for about 40 minutes, and between ⅙ and ⅐ h.p. for several hours at a time. The maximum horsepower from a highly trained male athlete for a burst of a few seconds seems to be a little less than 2 h.p. Interestingly, rowing a dinghy at a reasonable clip takes about ⅙ h.p.

Horsepower, Generated by Sail

In a Force 4 breeze (11 to 16 knots), 500 square feet of sail generates roughly 10 h.p. That's about 1 horsepower for every 50 square feet. Thus, a dinghy sail of 75 square feet generates about 1.5 h.p. Note, however, that if the wind speed doubles, horsepower is increased four times, not two times.

Horses, Live, Provisions for

In the days when navies had to transport horses on sailing ships, each horse was allowed 1,350 pounds of stores every five days. That makes it easier to understand why horses were sometimes thrown overboard in the tropical calms when water and provisions were running low—thus possibly giving the horse latitudes their name.

Hull Color, Best for Resale

Any color you like, as long as it's white.

Hull, Cost of

The hull, deck, and cabin of a normal monohulled yacht make up about one-third of the total finished cost of the vessel.

The implication here is that the savings in building a cheaper hull may not be as great as might be imagined, for they apply only to one third of the full price of the whole yacht.

Hull, Steel, Resale Value of
The resale value of a steel-hulled yacht drops by almost one-half after it reaches the age of 10 years.

There are many exceptions to this general rule, of course, but on the whole it holds good, as any experienced yacht broker will confirm.

Hurricane, Definition of
A hurricane is a storm of tropical origin reaching a strength of 64 knots (75 mph) or more. It starts off as a tropical depression, with winds of less than 33 knots. When wind speeds rise above 33 knots, it becomes a tropical storm.

Hurricanes, Avoidance Tactics
The most effective strategy for avoiding hurricanes is to keep well clear of the area during the hurricane season. However, any boat caught lying in the path of one will be in serious danger.

It's possible to increase the odds of survival by following certain rules. Both the hurricane and the tropical storm have two sides, or semicircles, known as the *dangerous* semicircle and the *navigable* semicircle—*navigable* being a purely comparative term, of course.

A small boat must try to place herself in the navigable semicircle. The dangerous semicircle lies on the right-hand side of the storm track in the Northern Hemisphere, facing the direction of its forward travel, and on the left side in the Southern Hemisphere.

Explicit directions for avoiding the most dangerous part of the storm are given in sailing instructions and many boating books, but basically boats caught to the right of, and in front of, a Northern Hemisphere storm should sail close-hauled on the starboard tack or heave-to on the starboard tack until the wind lifts and they can bear off and run at right angles away from the assumed track of the storm.

Boats caught in front of the other side, the navigable side, should run with the wind on the starboard quarter to make the best course they can at right angles to the storm track. The object in both cases is to put distance between the boat and the center of the hurricane.

How do you know where you are in relation to the hurricane's track? Well, you can locate the center of the storm with reasonable accuracy, but its actual track is either inspired guesswork or information received by radio or weatherfax.

If you face the wind in the Northern Hemisphere, the center of the storm is between 90 degrees and 135 degrees to your right, measuring from dead ahead. In the Southern Hemisphere, it's to your left.

If, on the northern side of the equator, you find the wind veering—that is, shifting direction clockwise—you're in the dangerous semicircle. If the wind backs, or swings counterclockwise, you're in the navigable semicircle.

If the wind direction stays constant, but the bottom falls out of the barometer and the wind speed increases, you are directly in its path.

If the wind direction stays constant, but the barometer is rising slowly and the wind speed is tapering off, you are directly behind the storm center.

The speed of advancement of the storm system as a whole along its track is usually about 10 knots in the early stages, but can increase drastically later on.

Hurricanes, When and Where Hurricanes feed on vapor from warm water, so their most active period is during late summer and fall when the water is at its warmest. In North American waters, hurricanes are experienced from May to November, and are most frequent in August, September, and October. The period from December to June is usually free of them. In the Far East, typhoons (hurricanes by another name) can form in any month, but most of them appear in late summer and early fall.

The areas most affected by these tropical revolving storms (also known as cyclones and willy-willies) are:

- The western North Atlantic
- The western North Pacific (Japan to Guam)
- The South Pacific (Marquesas to the Coral Sea)
- Australia's northern and northwestern coasts
- The Bay of Bengal
- The southwest Indian Ocean

Hypothermia, Diagnosis and Treatment of

Hypothermia, a dangerous lowering of the body's core temperature, is a threat in any water under 91 degrees F.

The colder the water, the quicker it happens. In water of 65 degrees F, a normal summertime temperature over most of the United States, a person without protective clothing can survive for about two hours before lapsing into unconsciousness.

Mild hypothermia is characterized by violent shivering, blue lips, and slurred speech. Get the victim out of cold water and wind, wrap him or her in warm dry clothes or bedding, and provide warm fluids, but no alcohol.

Medium hypothermia involves loss of muscle control, drowsiness, incoherent speech, and exhaustion—many of the symptoms of drunkenness. Now the victim is incapable of generating sufficient heat to warm up, so you must provide gentle, external, direct warmth. Sharing a sleeping bag is a good way. Simultaneous breathing into the victim's mouth as he or she breathes introduces warm air to the lungs. Do not massage arms and legs. It makes matters worse. Do not give the victim alcohol or stimulants such as coffee or tea.

Severe hypothermia involves collapse and unconsciousness, difficulty in breathing, and heart failure. It is a medical emergency and assistance should be sought if available. Treatment is the same as for medium hypothermia, with the likelihood that mouth-to-mouth resuscitation or cardiopulmonary resuscitation will be needed.

J

Jib Numbering and Naming System *Jibs*
(which to be absolutely worthy of the name should be
set flying from their own luffs) and *forestaysails* (or
foresails) are distinguished one from another by
their size. Thus, foresail No. 1 is the biggest, and No.
3 probably the working foresail.

Incidentally, a Genoa is a large forestaysail with a
low-cut, deck-sweeping foot, sheeted well aft of the
mast. A Yankee is another foresail, but with a high-
cut foot ending forward of the mast, and is often
flown in combination with a working forestaysail on
a cutter.

Aboard racing sailboats, foresails are often referred to by their size as a percentage of the fore triangle—that is, the triangle formed by the mast, the
forestay, and the foredeck. Thus, a 150-percent jib
would have area about 50 percent greater than that
of the foretriangle.

See also: FORESAILS, HEADSAILS, AND JIBS

Jib Sheet, Strain on To find the force applied
to the sheet by a jib or forestaysail, multiply the sail
area in square feet by the wind speed (in knots)
squared. Divide the answer by 232. This will give
you the approximate pull on the sheet in pounds.

K

Keel Bolts, Area of Keeping a heavy ballast keel snugly and safely in place in all weather requires that the keel bolts have a cross-sectional area of not less than 1 square inch for every 1,500 pounds of outside ballast.

This is valid for a fairly soft bolt material, such as bronze, having a tensile strength of not less than 60,000 pounds per square inch. Bolts made of stronger metal, such as Monel or stainless steel, can be correspondingly smaller.

See also: APPENDIX: TENSILE STRENGTHS OF MATERIALS USED IN BOATBUILDING

Keel Efficiency, Best Shape for For windward work, a deep, narrow keel is more efficient than is a wide, shallow keel. The leading edge should be a small radius or ellipse, with the maximum cross-sectional width about 35 to 45 percent of the keel length (that is, its fore-and-aft dimension, not depth) aft of the leading edge. The keel should be tapered smoothly to end in a feather edge—or, more practically, in a small radius.

Keels, Winged Winglets at the bottom of a keel cut down on induced drag and help get ballast low. But they also increase wetted surface (and thus friction drag), and they act as unwanted anchors when you run aground. They're an advantage only when you have a draft restriction. Most boats could be made equally efficient much more cheaply by simply having deeper ordinary keels. However, the patented Scheel keel appears to have most of the advantages of the winged keel without most of its disadvantages.

Knots, How Few You Really Need Most boaters have a stable of a few favorite knots that always stand them in good stead. But sometimes they suffer from a sneaking suspicion that a particular knot isn't really appropriate, and that they should know a fancier knot for that job. It might comfort them to know the old rule of thumb: If a simple knot can do the work, let it.

Here is a list of just 10 simple knots that, one way or another, will take care of all normal requirements aboard a boat: anchor bend, bowline, cleat hitch, clove hitch, figure eight, reef, rolling hitch, round turn and two half-hitches, timber hitch, sheet bend.

Some authorities advocate learning only three knots, three bends, and three hitches:

K

87

Knots: Figure eight, reef, and bowline

Bends: Double sheet, fisherman's, and topsail sheet

Hitches: Round turn and two half-hitches, clove, and rolling

But you can probably do almost everything you need to on a boat with just two knots, two bends, and one hitch—five in all:

- Anchor bend
- Bowline
- Reef knot
- Rolling hitch
- Topsail sheet bend

Knots, How to Tell a Good One Any knot that is to earn its keep aboard a boat must have three important attributes:

- It must hold fast under all conditions.
- It must come apart easily when you want it to.

- You must be able to make it almost automatically—that is, your finger muscles should be able to retain a "memory" of the knot and, with practice, form it quickly without thought, as one ties a necktie or a pair of shoelaces.

Another attribute of a good knot is that it can be tied or untied when the line is under strain.

Knots, Reduction in Strength of Line Any tight kink in a line diminishes its strength. In fact, any three-strand line that has suffered a severe kink can be assumed to have lost 30 percent of its strength. Some knots have tighter kinks than others, but all will cause a line to break more quickly under strain.

Here's how much the strength of rope is reduced by various knots:

Anchor bend: 24 percent

Round turn and two half-hitches: 30 to 35 percent

Timber hitch: 30 to 35 percent

Bowline: 40 percent

Clove hitch: 40 percent

Sheet bend: 45 percent

Reef knot: 55 percent

L

Lateral Plane, as a Percentage of Sail Area

Lateral plane area is what stops your boat from slipping sideways when the wind blows. Sail area is what tries to *make* it slip sideways. As a rule of thumb, the relation between the two can be expressed thus:

- The total lateral plane (including the rudder) of full-keeled boats should be between 12 and 16 percent of the sail area.
- The area of a fin keel (only) should be about 7 to 10 percent of sail area.
- The lateral plane area of a centerboard (only) can be as little as 5 percent of sail area.

Latitude, Approximate

The elevation, in degrees, of the North Star (*Polaris*) above the horizon is a rough approximation of the latitude (north of the equator) at that spot.

If *Polaris* were directly over the North Pole, its true altitude would be your latitude. But it can bear 2 degrees 6 minutes east or west of north. So, if you're reduced to finding your exact latitude from *Polaris*, be sure to apply the simple correction factor you'll find in any reputable nautical almanac.

Lead, Sounding

Nothing sounds more dated than the hoary advice that every cruising yacht should carry a 7-pound sounding lead on a 15- or 20-fathom line. Nevertheless, at the risk of being named a maritime Methuselah, I repeat it here. The advantage the lead has over the ubiquitous echo-sounder is that it is worked by gravity rather than electricity; and gravity, unlike electricity, is constantly available and always free. And—rather more to the point—the hollow in a lead can be armed with grease or soft soap to bring up a sample of the sea bed, which is often very useful knowledge. I'll say just one more thing: Plaited Dacron or Terylene is best for the line.

See also: APPENDIX: LEAD LINE MARKINGS (multiple entries)

Leaks, Emergency Actions to Take
Your chances of coping with a bad leak are directly proportionate to the amount of thought you have given beforehand to dealing with this emergency and the gear you have stowed away for the purpose.

Quite obviously, the priorities are to find the site (and cause) of the leak, and to stop it. This is far easier said than done, usually.

Boats and circumstances vary so widely that it would be impossible to set guidelines applicable in every case.

However, it usually pays to slow the boat down and employ all bilge pumps (and buckets) as soon as possible. If the water is flowing in faster than your pumps can handle it, make preparations to abandon ship.

But before you abandon, make an attempt to locate the site of the leak. Be ruthless. Rip away cabinet work with a crowbar where necessary. If you find the hole, you might be able to cover it from the outside with a collision mat or a sail. Try plugging it from the inside with a mattress backed by a locker door, jammed in place with an oar or boathook.

Send your Mayday before you lose battery power, but don't abandon ship before you have to.

See also: ABANDONING SHIP

Lee Helm, Effect of
Lee helm is not only dangerous and hard on the helmsman, it also increases resistance rapidly, far more than weather helm does,

even in the slightest amount. Don't live with lee helm any longer than you have to.

Leeway, in Sailboats Many factors affect leeway, but in general it can be assumed that a sailboat when close-hauled can make between 3 and 5 degrees of leeway in a 7-knot breeze. She can make between 5 and 8 degrees in a 20-knot breeze. This explains the old admonition to beginners that "she's not goin' where she's lookin'."

Lifelines, Height of The height of the upper lifelines, the wires running through stanchions placed at the edge of the deck, should never be less than 30 inches above deck. Guardrails or lifelines rigged much lower are good only for catapulting a person overboard. Sensible sailors going offshore, or in rough weather conditions, or even all the time, rig chest-high temporary lifelines of non-stretch Dacron, thus earning points for their Black Boxes (*q.v.*).

Incidentally, some confusion of terms still lingers here. In common usage, what used to be guardrails are now *lifelines*. What used to be lifelines, joining a personal harness to a strong point on the boat, are now *tethers*.

L

91

Liferaft, Chances of Survival in The survival chances are greater for a crew in a liferaft or lifeboat that can be sailed and steered.

Waiting passively to be rescued in a helplessly drifting liferaft is a prime cause of despair and hopelessness. According to Michael Stadler, a German professor of psychology and a small-boat sailor, "Even the most desperate situation is bearable, even for someone entirely on their own, provided they have some sense of having their position and environment under control."

See also: ABANDONING SHIP

Light, Jumping At night, a fixed or flashing point of light appears to jump around the horizon.

Sailors know this phenomenon well. Psychologists

call it the *autokinetic illusion*. It comes about through imperceptible eye movements or strain in the eye muscles when we stare fixedly at one point for too long. The light always reappears some distance to the left or right of where we expect it. Sometimes a lighthouse just lifting over the horizon appears to act like the stern light of a vessel ahead.

Lightning Protection, Principles of Lightning protection works by offering strikes a quick, easy, and safe path to take.

When you consider that a lightning flash can have an electrical potential of 30,000,000 volts and a current flow of 100,000 amps, it might seem suicidal to wish to *attract* strikes to your own mast or lightning antenna. But, as in love or war, attack often proves the best form of defense. A grounded conductor—that is, one in perfect electrical contact with the water—generally diverts to itself, and safely passes on, any lightning strike that would otherwise blow a hole through some other part of the boat or through you.

The area of protection is in the shape of a cone. The point is the top of your metal mast, or bare metal lightning conductor, and the base is a circle whose radius equals the height of the mast or conductor.

The ground must be of submerged metal with a surface area of no less than 1 square foot. A propeller or metal rudder can be used. Eric Hiscock maintains that emergency grounding, or earthing, can be achieved with a fathom or two of chain submerged in the water. I've done this myself in a fierce ocean lightning storm. I wrapped the chain around the backstay, which ran to the top of the metal mast, and let it trail in the boat's wake, with apparent success. But the path of the conductor (no less than a #8 gauge copper wire) should be as straight as possible with no sharp bends, otherwise the lightning might be tempted to take short cuts.

Incidentally, about two-thirds of lightning flashes strike from cloud to cloud and never reach the surface of the earth.

Chapman's Piloting, Seamanship and Small Boat Handling has more useful information, including a reminder that you shouldn't expect your lightning protection to work if you remove the boat from the water; unless, of course, you ground your ground, as it were.

Lights, Complex, Cautions Concerning

Don't trust a complex light unless you're well within its range.

Complex lights often show different colors over different sectors. But the rule of thumb is that the nominal range of a red or green light is between 15 and 30 percent less than that of a white light from the same navigational aid. Thus, at extreme range, you might misidentify a complex light because only its white light is visible.

Be cautious, too, when trying to use light sectors as an aid to navigation. Lights simply don't suddenly change from green to red when you cross a sector, as the chart might suggest. They shade gradually from one to the other while you cover a fair amount of ground. And sometimes, when you're about halfway between them, they'll appear a fainter white, because red and green light together make white light.

Lights, Faint, Locating
To find a faint light, such as a star, at night, look a little to one side, or above, or below where you expect to see it.

If you look straight at an object, the light rays focused by your eye fall on an area that is not as sensitive as the surrounding areas. So faint lights are often first seen in or toward the "corner" of the eye.

Lights at Sea, Distance Off
Never try to judge your distance from a single light at sea at night.

A single point of light provides no clues by which

our perceptions can judge its size and distance with any accuracy. Changes of size upon approach, and gradual increases in brightness, remain imperceptible to the human eye. In most cases, when the light is visibly nearer, you are in immediate danger of running into it.

Lines, Suggested Color Coding of

Most racing sailboats differentiate between different halyards, sheets, and control lines by color. Either the whole line is one color, or colored strands are woven into a mostly white line. Some cruising sailboats start out with similar good intentions, but after a few breakages and replacements the system is likely to deteriorate to the extent that only the owner understands the alleged color code. There is no single color code to which all sailors adhere, but here is a fairly common arrangement for all the control lines—sheets, halyards, topping lifts, and so forth—associated with any particular sail or system:

White: Mainsail
Blue: Jib and genoa
Red: Spinnaker
Green: Topping lifts
Orange: Vangs and travelers

Lines of Position, Permissible Angles

Two lines of position plotted on a chart should cross as near to 90 degrees as possible. For an acceptable fix, the angle between the two lines should never be less than 60 degrees or more than 120 degrees.

This is navigation de luxe, of course. On a small boat in bad conditions, you often have to make do with what you've got. The old rule of thumb is that any bearing is better than none. In practice, a fix from two lines intersecting at an angle as small as 30 degrees can be used if applied with a large dose of caution and common sense. Anything less than 30 degrees (or more than 150 degrees) is hardly worth plotting.

Log, Patent, Overhauling of
Some long-distance cruisers still carry a patent log for the accurate recording of daily distance run. It works by towing a small propeller, or spinner, through the water at the end of a line. The line turns a series of gears attached to pointers on the instrument's face. Streaming the log is easy; you simply drop it over the stern. Bringing the line in again, or overhauling the log, is more difficult and can lead to the most monumental tangles unless you know the rule. Simply detach the line at the inboard end before you start. Feed that end back into the water as you haul in, taking care to keep the incoming and outgoing parts well separated. When the spinner is in hand, you can easily recover the line with all the turns removed.

Log, Ship's Official
The rule of thumb is that nobody will ever ask to see your ship's log until you get into trouble.

It doesn't have to be professionally printed and bound in buffalo hide. A simple school notebook will do, with lines ruled for vertical columns.

It should provide an indication to a port captain or an Admiralty Court judge that your vessel is habitually run in a professional manner with due regard for national and international laws and the accepted practices of good seamanship.

Entries should be made regularly, at least at the end of each watch, and the skipper should sign each day's entries. Never make erasures. Strike through the incorrect entry without obliterating it, write the correct entry elsewhere, date it, and initial it.

M

Mainsail Slides, How to Attach A mainsail slide tends to jam in its track if it's seized too firmly to its cringle. When the sail is being hoisted, the fastening should be free to move to the top of the slide so the pull comes mostly from above. The opposite applies when the mainsail is being struck. A shackle of plastic or metal automatically provides this movement—at the cost of some periodic irritating rattling against the mast.

Making Fast, Correct Terms A vessel makes fast to the shore. She is not tied up. The old rule of thumb states that a boat makes fast *alongside* a jetty, pier, or wharf. She makes fast *in* a slip and *to* a buoy or pile.

Maneuvering a Sailboat in Gusty Weather There are frequent occasions when the requirements of navigation or the presence of other vessels makes it inconvenient to take in the reef a sailboat really needs. In such circumstances, it's often possible to follow the age-old advice:

> *In a puff, spring a luff,*
>
> *In a lull, keep her full.*

By alternately working to windward to feather the mainsail in the gusts and then falling well off to leeward in the lulls, you might be able to follow, on average, the course you require. This is a short-term expedient, of course, and the boat should be reefed and snugged down as soon as possible if any respectable distance remains to be covered.

Maneuvering a Strange Vessel Probably the most difficult maneuver a boater has to make in the normal course of events is to bring an unfamiliar boat alongside a pier or wharf for the first time.

Lacking all other knowledge of the boat's behavior, the general rule is to approach with the wharf on your port side at an angle of 10 to 20 degrees. Approach speed should be just above that at which steering control is lost.

Leave the rudder amidships, and when the bow is about 15 feet from the wharf, slip the transmission into astern gear, using the throttle as necessary to slow her down. This should swing her stern in tidily to the wharf, or at least leave you almost parallel to the wharf and close enough to heave lines ashore.

These instructions presume you have a right-handed propeller, which most are. If you know for sure you have a left-handed prop, approach with the wharf to starboard instead.

M

Note, too, that this is a very general rule, because there are too many possible variations of wind, current, traffic, and obstacles to formulate one specific approach. Nevertheless, if all other things were equal, this would be the basic approach to take. Adapt it as you must, according to the prevailing circumstances and your ability to pay for accident repairs.

Masts, Positions of

Cutter: One-third to one-half the waterline length abaft the stem

Sloop: One-quarter of the waterline length abaft the stem

Ketch: Mainmast about one-third of the waterline length aft of the stem; mizzenmast about one-sixth of the waterline length forward of the after end of the waterline

Yawl: Mainmast about one-fourth of the waterline length abaft the stem; mizzenmast on or very close to the after end of the waterline

Schooner: Foremast about 20 to 25 percent of the vessel's overall length abaft the stem; mainmast, 52 to 60 percent of the overall length abaft the stem.

A schooner's masts should not be set up parallel to each other. If they are, they appear to be closer together at the masthead than at deck level. The mainmast must rake slightly more than the foremast to compensate for this illusion.

Mast Sizes, Average
Keel-stepped standard aluminum section with a single spreader:

Crossways section (transverse): $\frac{1}{90}$ of the mast length from deck to headstay fitting

Fore-and-aft section: 1.4 times the crossways section

Wall thickness: $\frac{1}{35}$ of crossways section

For serious offshore cruising, increase crossways section by 10 to 15 percent and follow the rule of thumb through as before.

Double spreader rig: As for single spreader, but after calculating all dimensions, reduce the transverse or crossways section (only) by 10 to 15 percent.

Deck-stepped masts (weaker): Use the same rule of thumb as for keel-stepped masts, but divide mast length by 85 instead of 90.

Always round *up* to the nearest fraction of an inch.

Mechanical Similitude, Law of
Fascinating things start to happen when you vary the size of a boat. The law of mechanical similitude works like this for boats that are similar in shape:

If you double the size of a vessel evenly all around:

- Length increases by 2 times
- Beam increases by 2 times
- Draft increases by 2 times
- Wetted surface area increases by 4 times

- Volume increases by 8 times
- Weight increases by 8 times
- Stability increases by 16 times

The new boat, supposedly just double the size of the old one, would actually be 41 percent faster, able to carry four times as much sail, eight times heavier, eight times roomier below, and 16 times more stable.

No right-minded person would actually build a boat to the new dimensions, of course, but it helps explain why large sailing yachts are so much stiffer than small ones, even if they carry proportionately less beam and draft.

This law also explains why you can't just take a set of plans for a 25-footer and enlarge them 200 percent to build a 50-footer. As a boat gains length, she needs *proportionately* less beam and less draft because she gains stability so rapidly. The rule of thumb is that long boats are skinnier than short boats.

Miles, Converting Nautical to Statute
Multiply nautical miles by 1.15. (Or, multiply by 8 and divide by 7.)

Miles, Converting Statute to Nautical
Multiply statute miles by 0.875. (Or multiply by 7 and divide by 8.)

Miles, Definitions of The exact length of a nautical mile has varied with mankind's ability to measure the earth. It's the equivalent of $\frac{1}{60}$ of 1 degree (which in itself is $\frac{1}{360}$ of the distance around the earth if you travel a great circular route going through both poles). For all practical purposes, 1 degree of latitude equals 60 nautical miles. Thus, 1 minute of latitude (which is $\frac{1}{60}$ of one degree) equals 1 nautical mile.

Reducing this to feet has proved a more formida-

M

99

ble task. For many years the nautical mile was measured as 6,080 feet. Now, with the latest scientific help, the figure has been changed to 6,076.1 feet, or 2,025.4 yards.

Practical sailors can simplify their lives enormously by ignoring all this overfinicky fine-tuning and using in their calculations a nautical mile of 2,000 yards, one-tenth of which (the good old cable) is 200 yards. It's as near as dammit and about as good as navigation gets aboard a small boat.

The ever faithful statute, or land, mile of 5,280 feet or 1,760 yards is the one mariners use on the Great Lakes, inland rivers, and the Intracoastal Waterway.

Motions of a Sailboat at Sea

The well-known naval architect and author Francis S. Kinney asserted that there were eight motions of a sailboat at sea:

Broaching: Accidentally swinging broadside to the wind and sea when running free.

Heaving: Rising and falling as a whole with the seas.

Pitching: Plunging so that the bow and stern rise and fall alternately.

Pitchpoling: Accidentally tumbling stern-over-bow in a half-forward somersault.

Rolling: Inclining rhythmically from side to side.

Surging: Being accelerated and decelerated by overtaking swells.

Swaying: Moving bodily sideways.

Yawing: Lurching and changing direction to either side of the proper course.

Motorsailer, Definition of

Presume a headwind of Force 6 (22 to 27 knots) and short, choppy seas. If a sailboat could make way to windward quicker under shortened sail than under her motor alone, she is an auxiliary sailing yacht. If she could reach her windward destination quicker by keeping going under power alone, she is a motorsailer.

This definition by Francis S. Kinney, in *Skene's Elements of Yacht Design*, cites the condition of strong breeze and heavy sea head-on as the dividing line between sailing auxiliaries and motorsailers.

However, as modern auxiliary engines become more and more powerful for the same size and weight, that line becomes increasingly blurred.

Multihulls, Speed of

Catamarans, trimarans, and proas rely on light weight, large sail areas, and great stability to give them their speed.

Whereas a monohull's considerable beam and draft create form resistance, a catamaran, for example, has knife-like hulls that slip through the water with little tendency to make waves.

As a displacement monohull speeds up, she finds herself trapped in one big wave of her own making, a wave just a little longer than the boat itself. A non-planing boat of this type cannot leap up and over the front part of the wave and she cannot go any faster than the wave, whose speed in knots is 1.34 times the square root of the distance in feet between crests.

So, whereas a heavy displacement monohull's maximum speed is limited to 1.34 times the square root of her waterline length, a catamaran, drawing great stability from her widely spaced hulls, and therefore able to carry much more sail, can often reach speeds twice or three times those of a monohull of the same waterline length.

A trimaran or proa might have a hull shape more akin to that of a monohull, but also gains the extra stability afforded by an outrigger or amas, and therefore greater power from the wind.

Cruising catamarans often fail to come up to

their owner's expectations of speed because their potential is more severely curtailed by extra displacement than is a monohull's. Cruisers are notorious for carting around every luxury they can cram aboard, and this sybaritic lifestyle robs comparatively more speed from multihulls than it does from monohulls, which are not quite so sensitive to power-to-weight ratios after a certain limit has been reached.

Multihulls, Stability of

By virtue of their wide beam, multihulled craft enjoy enormous initial stability. Interestingly, however, they are as stable upside down as they are rightside up.

If a multihull's initial stability is overcome by a sudden, extra-strong gust of wind, or by wave action, and she capsizes through 180 degrees, she will stay that way unless emergency righting procedures are put into effect.

Most importantly, though, she will not sink, because, unlike a monohull, she does not carry a heavy ballast keel for stability. She will continue to provide flotation and shelter for her crew. She won't be capable of going anywhere, of course, except where the current takes her, and this is a very good reason why all offshore multihulls should carry EPIRBs.

Some multihulls carry flotation at the masthead to prevent their capsizing through a full 180 degrees, though this of itself does not guarantee quick recovery to a normal position. Others are capable of flooding one hull in the capsized position to aid recovery (and pumping it dry afterwards) or have other ingenious ways of righting the craft.

Multihulls are perfectly capable of roaming the oceans of the world if their crews are alert and experienced and if all the safeguards against accidental capsize are in working order. Whether or not they qualify for the ultimate definition of seaworthiness on the open ocean, which is that a vessel left entirely to her own devices should at all times be capable of looking after herself and an incapacitated crew, is the subject of seemingly endless, and often pointless, debate. After all, most monohulls would fail that test, too.

N

Name, Attracting Bad Luck with A vessel with a name that is too presumptuous has long been held to attract bad luck.

By presumptuous, I mean a name that challenges the sea or the wind, or boasts that it can better the elements or survive their meanest blows. To call a boat *Sea Conqueror* or *Wind Tamer* is simply to tempt the Fates. The gods like boat names to be humble.

To call a ship *Titanic* is asking for trouble, too. In Greek mythology, the most important of the 12 Titans, the vengeful Kronos, cut off his father's genitals with a sickle, and threw them into the sea. I can imagine how Neptune, god of the sea, would feel about a ship named after the Titans. Of course, the *Titanic* was ill-fated from the start anyway—she was launched without a naming ceremony, thus greatly offending the gods.

Name, Changing of It's not unlucky to change the name of a boat, provided certain rules are followed, including the holding of Vigor's little-known interdenominational de-naming ceremony.

The first requirement is to remove the old name from everything on board. Take the old log book ashore. Check for offending books and charts with the name inscribed. Be ruthless. Sand away the old name from the transom, topsides, and dinghy. Painting over it is not sufficient. Remove and replace a name carved into wood or, at the very minimum, fill with putty and paint over.

Concoct your own ceremony, to be performed with or without spectators. Make it short, sweet, and simple. The elements of the ceremony are twofold: a supplication and a libation. Address directly the gods of the wind (Aeolus), sea (Neptune), and any others you want, and ask them to strike from their records the old name of the boat. Mention the name. Then pray their indulgence in extending their goodwill and protection to the vessel in her new name, which will be revealed in a separate naming ceremony to come. Do not mention the new name.

Then, without further words, pour a libation of champagne, the best you can afford, over the bows. Be generous. You may drink some yourself and offer some to your guests, if any, but don't be mean with the gods' portion or you'll regret it. And unless you're absolutely bent on self-destruction, don't use a cheap substitute for real champagne. Remember, the champagne represents the blood sacrifice of the ancients. It saves you from having to slaughter your favorite virgin, so don't stint on the price.

Immediately thereafter, or at any interval to suit yourself, you may conduct a normal naming ceremony as if she were a brand-new vessel. And yes, since blood sacrifice is no longer encouraged or even tolerated, you do need another, fresh bottle of champagne. Real champagne.

I have changed the name of a boat in this way with great success, and I can recommend Vigor's interdenominational de-naming ceremony to all without hesitation.

N

105

Navigation, Britain to Caribbean
The old rule of thumb was: "South 'til the butter melts, then west." It still works if, like many European sailors, you don't have a fridge.

Navigation, Difficulty of
Despite the best efforts of generations of navigators to make it appear

otherwise, navigation aboard small boats is neither difficult nor mysterious.

As three-time circumnavigator Eric Hiscock put it: "Setting the course, keeping the dead reckoning up to date, and fixing the position by observations of the celestial bodies, call for nothing more than simple arithmetic, a little geometry, and some dexterity in handling the sextant."

Navigation, Emergency The best advice is: Read about it now. Worry about it when it happens.

Like most deep-sea sailors, I have read with great fascination books on emergency navigation. But I have come to the conclusion that much of it is plain common sense, some of it depends entirely on luck (what instruments and tables are left available to you), and the rest is rooted too deeply in the actual science of navigation for my liking.

It is indeed fascinating to understand the movements of the heavenly bodies and to use mathematical formulas to make them divulge information of use to you, but it requires more study than I am prepared to devote to it.

Deep-sea voyaging covers so many different disciplines, from medicine and aerodynamics to culinary arts and mechanical engineering, that there just isn't time in one human lifespan to plunge headlong into the depths of each and every one.

Anyone with common sense, a reasonable amount of reading, a broad-based education in the arts and sciences, and enough experience to attempt an ocean crossing, should be able to fathom a way back to land if it's at all possible.

If I were forced to make a choice, I would rather devote time to studying survival techniques than emergency navigation. The ability to catch fish, find plankton, and gather fresh water might be worth far more to a sailor than a deep knowledge of navigation.

This is purely a personal observation, of course, and in no way diminishes the value of reading books on emergency navigation (which every deep-sea sailor should do), nor the added pleasure, interest, and satisfaction it can bring to a voyage.

Perhaps what this all boils down to is confidence. Like many other sailors, I grew up in small dinghies, often at sea, and I have never doubted my ability to sail one to safety across an ocean in an emergency.

Possibly this confidence is misplaced, but it's there. And as long as I feel I can sail toward a large piece of land that I can't possibly miss, surviving indefinitely off the sea, I don't really need to study in any great depth the very fine techniques of emergency navigation that might—or might not—guide me to the safety of a smaller but nearer island.

Navigation Lights, Specifications for

Fit the brightest lights for which you have power or battery capacity. Colored glass absorbs 85 to 90 percent of the light from the bulb.

With a 12-volt system and lights showing through *clear glass or plastic* in the most favorable weather conditions:

- A 24-watt bulb is visible at about three miles.

- A 12-watt bulb is visible at about two miles.

- Showing through *red or green glass or plastic* in the most favorable weather conditions:

- A 24-watt bulb is visible at a little over 1 mile.

It is interesting to note that to increase visibility from 3 to 4 miles, the brightness of a lamp must be *doubled*.

See also: ANCHOR LIGHT, REQUIRED SIZE

O

Oars, Dinghy If you paint or varnish your dinghy oars, leave the handles bare, otherwise they'll be too slippery when wet. Varnish is good for giving visible evidence of the condition of the wood, but it's a devil to keep up. Paint, particularly white paint, is more practical, but hides faults. Ash is hard and durable, but heavy. Spruce is 35 percent lighter and doesn't rot easily, but is soft and wears easily without protection. All dinghy oar blades benefit from straps of copper or fiberglass around the blades to prevent their splitting and to lessen the wear of contact with the ground, jetties, the mother yacht, and the occasional bather.

Oars, Size of For serious rowers in a boat specifically designed to be rowed, the correct length of an oar is governed by the span across the beam of the boat between oarlocks. First find the inboard length of the oar by taking one-half of the span and adding two inches. Then the total length of the oar is $\frac{1}{7}$ of the inboard length, multiplied by 25. The distance from the center of the leather to the end of the handle is $\frac{7}{25}$ of the total length of the oar.

This results in an oar longer than that needed for the usual yacht tender, for which a "lower gear" often is required for windward work. The simpler rule of thumb for tenders is that the overall length of each oar should be about 1½ times the distance between the oarlocks. Thus, for a tender with a 4-foot beam, 6-foot oars would suffice.

Ocean, Main Constituents of Ever wondered
what's in seawater besides ordinary common salt?
Here's a list showing the number of grams of various substances in every kilogram (1,000 grams) of
water at a salinity of 35 percent:

Chloride	19.4
Sodium	10.8
Sulphate	2.7
Magnesium	1.3
Calcium	0.4
Potassium	0.4
Bicarbonate	0.1
Bromide	0.067
Strontium	0.008
Boron	0.004
Fluoride	0.001

O

109

Ocean, Mean Temperatures As a rule, oceans
in the Southern Hemisphere are considerably colder
than those north of the equator. Here are rough
average temperatures in degrees Fahrenheit for
three oceans in both hemispheres at different latitudes:

	Northern Hemisphere		
Latitude	Atlantic	Pacific	Indian
0 to 10	80	81	82
10 to 20	79	79	82
20 to 30	76	74	79
30 to 40	69	66	—
40 to 50	56	50	—
50 to 60	48	42	—
60 to 70	42	—	—

| | Southern Hemisphere | | |
Latitude	Atlantic	Pacific	Indian
0 to 10	77	79	81
10 to 20	74	77	78
20 to 30	70	71	73
30 to 40	62	62	63
40 to 50	48	52	48
50 to 60	35	41	35
60 to 70	30	30	30

Ocean, Salts Present in

These are the average percentages of all the salts found in sea water:

Sodium chloride	$NaCl$	77.8
Magnesium chloride	$MgCl_2$	10.9
Magnesium sulphate	$MgSO_4$	4.7
Calcium sulphate	$CaSO_4$	3.6
Potassium sulphate	K_2SO_4	2.5
Calcium carbonate	$CaCO_3$	0.3
Magnesium bromide	$MgBr_2$	0.2

Ocean Voyaging, Size of Boat for

The larger the vessel the better for ocean voyaging, according to Eric Hiscock, provided her management is within the capabilities of her crew and within their financial scope. In other words, a good big boat is better than a good small boat.

In practice, most couples find a boat of about 30 feet, with moderate to heavy displacement, about right for their physical capabilities. The great majority of sailboats that have been cruising for three years or more are within a few feet either way of 30 feet on deck. Hiscock and his wife, Susan, moved up to bigger boats, but never seemed as happy with them as they had been with the 30-foot *Wanderer III*, in which they twice circumnavigated the world.

Oceangoing Sailboat, Basic Requirements for

In order of importance, the basic needs of an oceangoing yacht are: seaworthiness, comfort, self-steering ability, and speed.

Seaworthiness includes stability and self-righting characteristics as well as brute strength. It also supposes the ability to claw off a lee shore in heavy weather, and the ability to lie ahull or heave to safely when unattended.

Oil, Color of Marine engineers seem to be of one mind in this: Used engine oil should be jet black, and no other color. If, after some hours of use, it's brown, milky, or some other color, seek expert advice as soon as possible.

Osmosis *See*: BLISTERING OF FIBERGLASS HULLS

Outboard Motors, Reviving Drowned

The rule of thumb for outboards dropped in sea water is to render first aid immediately, because corrosion sets in within three hours.

If you believe sand might have been drawn into the engine, or if you can hear grating and grinding when you turn the flywheel, you must either disassemble the engine or call for expert help after thoroughly hosing everything down with fresh water.

O

111

Otherwise, proceed as follows:

1. Rinse all salt water away with fresh water. Do not be scared to douse everything, including electrics.

2. Remove and dry the spark plugs.

3. Remove, clean, and dry the carburetor.

4. With the plug hole facing downward to drain, turn the engine over several times.

5. Squirt light engine oil into the cylinders.

6. Replace the carburetor and plugs.

7. Start the engine.

If necessary, remove the plugs, dry any remaining moisture, and try again. Inspect the carburetor once more for water. Keep trying to start it. Be persistent. When it runs, let it get good and warm to dry out—and give yourself a well-deserved pat on the back.

If the beast simply refuses to start, try to submerge it in fresh water until you can summon more skilled help.

Outboard Motors, Twin, Disadvantages of

A single outboard motor is more economical than two outboard motors half the size.

Two motors are safer than one, especially for off-shore work. But a twin rig with the same power as a single motor costs about 30 to 40 percent more and weighs about 50 percent more. It needs additional battery capacity. It has more complex control systems. Underwater drag is increased, and fuel consumption goes up by 30 to 50 percent.

A more sensible rig in many cases is to have a single outboard motor of full power, with a much smaller motor for use as an emergency backup or for slow-speed trolling.

To be truly reliable, the backup motor should have a totally separate fuel supply, since the most frequent cause of outboard failure is fuel contaminated by dirt or water. Twin motors drawing fuel from the same tank will be knocked out as fast as a single.

Overhangs, Dangers of

Long overhangs on sailboat hulls look elegant and serve the purpose of lengthening the load waterline when the boat heels, thus increasing her speed potential. But they're best suited to sheltered waters and have no place on a seagoing cruiser. Excessive overhangs cause pounding at the bow and slamming at the stern. In quartering seas, the leverage afforded by a long overhang allows the overtaking swell to spin the boat broadside on into a dangerous broaching position. Remember the rule: long overhang, calm water.

Overloading, the Safety Limit It's easy to overload a boat without realizing it, thus reducing safety margins of stability and flotation. In general, however, average-displacement yachts may be allowed to rise or sink above their design waterlines an amount equal to 1 percent of their waterline length.

See also: DINGHY, HARD, CAPACITY OF

O

P

Paint, Antifouling Antifouling paint discourages the growth of barnacles and plant life on the submersed hull of your boat. If you have a wooden boat, antifouling also discourages marine borers from eating it for lunch. As a rule, copper in one form or another has been, and still is, the most-favored biocide.

For some years, tin (tributyltin, or TBT) was found to be more effective, but its harmful effects on shellfish led to its banning for most marine applications by the U.S. Congress in 1988.

So now it's back to copper, and the rule of thumb is that the more copper a paint contains, the more effective an antifoulant it is.

There are four basic ways to apply copper-loaded paints to the bottoms of boats:

- Apply a paint that slowly dissolves over time, exposing fresh copper as it does so.

- Use a harder paint that allows the biocide to diffuse through its skin.

- Use one of the newer copolymer paints that act by hydrolysis, or chemical reaction with water, and the scouring action of water flowing past the hull.

- Apply a thick (12 to 15 mil) coat of resin, polyester or epoxy, in which countless millions of tiny pieces of copper metal are suspended, each one individually coated with an extremely thin coat of resin and thus electrically insulated from its mates.

In this last system, new copper is exposed by scrubbing the hull every few months. It's possible that this method can last the life of the boat, but application is a job best left to the professionals.

For most boats in most areas, the copolymer type, which can last as long as four years, is the most effective of the three antifouling coats you can apply yourself. And—wouldn't you know it?—it's the most expensive of the three.

Paint, Estimating Areas to Cover
Measurements in feet, answers in square feet:

Topsides: Length overall plus beam times 2 times average freeboard.

Bottom: Load waterline times beam times draft. For full-keel cruising sailboats, take ¾ of this figure. For light-displacement sailboats, take ½ of the area.

Decks: Length overall times beam times 0.75 (minus area of cockpit and deck structures).

Spars: Length times 2½ times average diameter.

Refer to the paint cans or manufacturer's brochures for the amount of paint needed to cover square footage. Modern paint finishes vary widely in their covering capacity. The old rule of thumb was that a gallon of enamel paint or varnish would cover 500 square feet; antifouling topcoat would cover 350 to 400 square feet per gallon.

P

115

Paint, Polyurethane, Amateur Application of
Many boat owners don't believe that two-part polyurethane paint can be slapped on a hull with a brush or rolled on by amateurs in much the same way as any other paint.

The mystique that has sprung up around twin-pack polyurethane seems to have convinced too many boaters that it can be applied only by those with master's degrees in nuclear physics or applied chemistry or whatever discipline is responsible for linking all those copolymeric molecules in that striking linear way.

I started using fiberglass and polyester resin on stitch-and-glue boats way back in 1967, so when two-part polyurethane paint came along I just bought it and used it without thinking. It was expensive, and it was tricky to use, but no more tricky than fiberglass.

I brush-painted the topsides of my 28-foot C & C racer in one day on my own and she looked beautiful. This is not the place for a treatise on painting, but the real trick is to paint fast, with horizontal strokes, in vertical sections between 12 and 18 inches wide.

In other words, you paint in thin strips from the gunwale to the waterline. Then you start the next strip 18 inches to the left (if you're right-handed) and fair the new paint into the still-wet edge of the old strip as you go down. Maintaining a wet edge is the big secret.

Or perhaps the real secret is not to be afraid of the stuff. You can always sand it down with waterproof paper if you make a mess of it. Try it. You might surprise yourself—and save a small fortune.

Painting, Best Time of Day for One old rule of thumb says you shouldn't paint or varnish anything out in the open before 10 AM or after 4 PM.

But you can bend the rules if you *know* the rules. And the rules vary, of course, with different kinds of paint, or "protective coating systems," as they like to call them now. So whether you've got the kind of paint that dries by solvent evaporation or the kind that hardens by the chemical cross-linking of molecules, the first rule is to read the instructions that come with your can of paint, bearing in mind these general principles that apply to almost all kinds of paint or varnish:

The work to be covered must be smooth, clean, dry, and free of anything that is likely to prevent paint from sticking to it. It must also have been prepared correctly—that is, it should have been primed, filled, and undercoated, and anything else the manufacturer thought necessary to receive the kind of coating you're contemplating applying.

The temperature must be reasonably mild so the paint can transform itself from a liquid to a hard skin without getting so hot that it forms blisters or so cold that it freezes or dries without a shine.

"Reasonably mild" in most cases means somewhere between 60 and 80 degrees F, but only your paint manufacturer can confirm that. It's possible to paint when it's quite a lot colder or hotter, and I've done it. Sometimes you have no choice but to play the hand Nature deals you, and just take a chance. After enough painting, you develop a feeling for what you can get away with.

Starting at 10 AM gives the day a chance to warm up. It allows the dew to dry. Stopping at 4 PM gives the paint a chance to skin over before the air begins to cool down and dew begins to form. Water coming into contact with most uncured paint affects its looks, if not its integrity. It could dry without a shine. Varnish could develop milky blotches.

P

117

But the 10 to 4 rule is really just for beginners. Many different factors affect it, especially your latitude and the season of the year. The more experience you gain in painting, the more you'll feel confident about bending the rule.

When you do, remember: It's on *your* head.

Passages and Gangways, Dimensions of

Boats come in a wider variety of shapes and sizes than human beings do. But even on the smallest boat there should be a reasonable amount of space for human beings to move around in.

The minimum width for passages and doorways down below is 19 inches. Below the waist, you can get away with a cutout only 14 inches wide. The waist is usually taken to be 30 inches above the floor.

If you have the space, 24-inch-wide passages and doorways are about right.

Performance, Human, Variation with Time of Day
Human performance levels drop steeply between midnight and 3 AM. They peak between 6 AM and 11 AM, and then taper off again until 3 PM, after which there is a gradual improvement to average levels at 5 PM.

On short trips, during which the crew has had no chance to become accustomed to night watches, it's advisable to make the watches as short as possible between midnight and 4 AM. Industrial psychologists have found it takes six to eight days for factory workers to become accustomed to new shifts.

Planing, Angle of Minimum Resistance
When a powerboat is planing, the minimum resistance lies between 2 and 4 degrees of trim by the stern.

Planing, Definition of
Mathematically speaking, planing occurs when speed, in miles per hour, divided by the square root of the waterline length in feet, equals 2 or more. For example, a 25-foot-waterline length boat theoretically begins planing at 10 miles an hour.

Planing, Speed to Initiate, in Dinghies
In practice, the speed in knots at which most small sailing dinghies start planing can be found by multiplying the square root of the waterline length in feet by 2.2.

Planking, Sizes of, for Wooden Boats
Roughly speaking, you can determine the proper thickness of planking by the length of the hull:

10-foot boat: ¼-inch planking

20-foot boat: ½-inch planking

40-foot boat: 1-inch planking

Plankton, as Survival Food

Under survival conditions, drag an old shirt like a net through the water at night—not during the day, because most plankton avoid the sun and even strong moonlight. A towing speed of about two knots is about right. The great percentage of crustaceans makes plankton a rich, nourishing food, even raw.

Ocean scientist William Beebe asserted in 1927 that "ship-wrecked men in an open boat, if their lot is cast on waters rich in plankton, need never starve to death." This was proved true in 1952 when Frenchman Dr. Alain Bombard drifted across the Atlantic from Casablanca in his rubber liferaft *L'Hérétique* without food or water, existing on fish and plankton he caught in a fine net.

Some people warn you not to eat plankton because some of it, such as the red tide, is poisonous. The red tide is a reddish discoloration of the sea caused by red protozoan flagellates—little critters that kill fishes and other creatures by releasing poisons. Obviously, even if you're starving, you should avoid eating the red tide.

P

119

Plywood Decks, Spacing of Beams for

Ever watched from your bunk as a crewmember lurched across the plywood deck above your head? Ever wondered if it was meant to buckle that much? It shouldn't, if the spacing of the deck beams is correct. Here's the old rule:

Plywood thickness	Beam spacing
¼ inch	5¾ inches
⅜ inch	8 inches
½ inch	10 inches
⅝ inch	12 inches
¾ inch	14 inches

Porthole, Definition of

A porthole is an opening in the hull to admit light and air. It's also known as a *port*. The framed glass used to make the porthole watertight has two names: If it can be opened it's called a *portlight*; if not, it's a *deadlight*.

Position Determination, Frequency of

Learner navigators often ask, "How often is it necessary to fix the ship's position?" The rule is that there is no rule, other than to use plain common sense.

If you're feeling your way along a channel in fog, checking the number of each buoy against the chart as you pass it, you're quite rightly keeping a full-time position plot. In mid-ocean, on the other hand, it's rarely necessary to fix your position more than once a day. In between, there are a variety of situations that call for common-sense judgment.

Just remember, it's the skipper's duty to know the approximate position of the ship at all times, in case he or she needs to call for help. With that in mind, the frequency of fixing position and/or updating the dead reckoning should work itself out. The proximity of hazards obviously affects that frequency, as does a responsible skipper's tendency to secure a fix at every opportunity whether it's needed or not—and thereby earn points for the Black Box (*q.v.*).

Pounds per Inch Immersion *See*: WATERPLANE AREA

Powerboats, Atkin's Suggestions for The
famous designer William Atkin proposed the following desirable design features for motorboats:

For tidal rivers

• High freeboard

• Generous flam and flare

• Protected propeller and rudder

• More than average speed

For lakes

• High freeboard

- Plenty of topside flare
- More than average draft

For deep water

- Lower than average freeboard
- Modest topside flare
- Moderate speed
- Deep draft

For a Florida bayou

- Shallow draft
- Shade awnings, insect screens, and generous ventilation
- A standing top

For the coast of Maine

- Strong and seaworthy hull
- Snug cabin
- Efficient stove

Preventers, Manifold Uses of The rule of thumb is that an ounce of preventer is worth a pound of cure.

Preventers prevent from happening things that *shouldn't* happen. They can therefore be used as a measure of a skipper's forethought and ability to anticipate the worst.

Preventers prevent the mainsail from jibing accidentally and causing the mast to fall down. Preventers hold dinghies firmly to the cabintop and prevent their disappearance overboard in storms. Preventers act as backups to lines under great strain, thus minimizing any damage that might occur and turning major catastrophes into minor inconveniences.

Preventers, more often than not, are simply pieces of fiber or wire rope, intelligently placed and artfully attached in the right place at the right time to stop something awful from happening.

Many, such as the topping lift, are permanent and known by other names. Others are temporary and applied as the need arises. But the best ships carry the most preventers, because wise skippers know preventers are worth points in the Black Box (*q.v.*).

Price, to Convert for Cruising Preparing a new production boat for extended cruising costs about an additional 25 percent of its purchase price. A second-hand boat already used for cruising costs less—about 10 to 15 percent extra.

Price Apportionment, Yard-Built Yacht
When calculating the price of a new yacht you can figure on:

- 30 percent for materials
- 50 percent for labor
- 20 percent for the yard's overhead expenses

However, long experience has shown that the prospective owner should be prepared for a 10- to 20-percent overrun of the total estimated cost for unforeseen contingencies.

Price per Pound, New Cruising Sailboat
For the top-quality materials and workmanship demanded by a transoceanic cruising yacht, the builders' charge in 1993 was about $6 to $8 per pound of displacement.

This price was for a new fiberglass production boat, theoretically in sailaway condition but lacking many items of gear that seasoned cruisers would deem essential.

Privacy, the Need for Every crewmember needs a place aboard where he or she is guaranteed privacy.

This is difficult under the normally crowded conditions on a yacht, but becomes more important with the length of the passage. A bunk is the most suitable spot, and a personal curtained-off pilot berth is many sailors' dream of heaven. It's important that crewmembers respect and preserve each other's private retreats, as well as any small stowage spaces allocated to them.

Propeller, Efficiency of A large-diameter, slow-turning propeller is usually more efficient than a small one turning at high speed. The exception to this rule is the boat that operates at 35 knots or more. (In small craft, slow-turning usually means fewer than 1,000 revolutions per minute.)

All propellers lose efficiency because of slippage in the water. Roughly speaking, the slippage of propellers on certain types of boats is as follows:

High-speed powerboats: About 20 percent

Light power cruisers: About 24 percent

Heavy power cruisers: About 26 percent

Auxiliary sailboats: Between 40 and 55 percent

Propeller, Handedness A propeller that screws forward when it revolves clockwise, as seen from astern, is known as a *right-handed* propeller. Most single propellers are right-handed, but twin installations have one right-handed and one left-handed propeller to neutralize their respective sideways thrusts.

Propeller, Shaft Sizes Here is a rule of thumb for finding the size of propeller shaft needed in small craft. For a Tobin bronze shaft, divide propeller diameter by 14.5 for a two-bladed propeller, by 14.0 for three blades, and by 13.1 for four blades. For a stronger stainless steel shaft, diameters can be 10 percent less than those for bronze. For a Monel shaft, divide propeller diameter by 18.1 for two blades, by 17.5 for three blades, and by 16.3 for four blades. The results are in inches.

Propeller, Walking Sideways

At low speeds, particularly, a propeller tends to walk sideways through the water as if it were a wheel. The effect is more marked in reverse because the rudder is usually less efficient at correcting the sideways torque then. As a rule, a right-handed propeller going astern tends to push the boat's stern to port—that is, to *your* right as you face *aft*.

Propellers, Types of

Why are some propellers two-bladed and some three-bladed? Why are some fixed, some feathering, and some folding?

It's all a question of compromise. In the sizes, and at the speeds, usually found in auxiliary sailboats with fixed propellers, a two-bladed prop is often the most efficient.

But sometimes there just isn't sufficient clearance between the shaft and the hull to accommodate those long thin blades. So the load is spread among three broader blades of smaller diameter. Each blade here is working in water slightly more disturbed by its predecessor than a two-bladed prop would be, so it's slightly less efficient.

But a three-bladed prop is less prone to vibration than is a two-bladed one, and needs less of a hole cut in the rudder, if that's the way it's fitted.

A two-bladed prop, on the other hand, can be nicely lined up vertically behind the rudder post and so avoid much of the drag of a three-bladed prop. And so it goes. In the end, the best advice is probably to fit a two-bladed prop if you can, a three-bladed one if you can't, and stop worrying about it.

A folding prop causes very little drag, but is prone not to open at all if a fat barnacle grows in the wrong place. So folding props are more suited to racing yachts than to cruisers. Folding props can be tricky in reverse and sometimes need a transmission with a higher than normal astern gear ratio to make them open properly.

Adjustable pitch props require no gearbox or clutch but are quite rare, presumably because the sophisticated mechanism needed to vary the pitch under way is expensive and more prone to malfunction than are a simple prop and gearbox.

An automatic feathering prop, such as the Max-Prop, reduces drag while sailing, but its fine engineering makes it too expensive for most cruising yachts, which happily drag fixed, reliable three-bladed props around the oceans of the world.

Propellers, Various Handy Facts

- The question of whether a freely rotating propeller creates less drag than one that is fixed still causes confusion. U.S. naval architect and author Dave Gerr asserts, "The simple answer is that a propeller creates less drag when free to rotate." But, he adds, if you can hide a two-bladed propeller from the flow of water by locking it vertically behind a skeg or keel, it produces less drag than when freely rotating.

P

125

On the other hand, British sailor and author Eric Hiscock writes, "Experiments made by P. Newall Petticrow Ltd. have shown that a 2- or 3-bladed propeller offers less drag when it is locked than when it is free to spin, and that the drag of a spinning propeller is greatest at about 100 r.p.m."

Francis S. Kinney, in *Skene's Elements of Yacht Design*, agrees with Hiscock: "The shaft should be locked so that the propeller cannot revolve. It has been found that a revolving propeller creates more drag...."

Most practical sailors conclude from this that it doesn't make much difference what you do, since the advantage or disadvantage does not appear to be great enough even for experts to measure easily. There's one point to watch, though: Not all transmission systems can lubricate a free-spinning shaft.

- Increased diameter absorbs more power than increased pitch.

- A decrease of one inch in diameter is good for an increase of about 300 revolutions per minute.

- On auxiliary sailboats, absolute minimum clearance between hull and blade tips is 10 percent of propeller diameter. On powerboats, 20-percent clearance or more is usually needed to prevent vibration.

- The thinner lock nut should be installed on the propeller shaft directly against the propeller hub. As the larger, second nut is tightened, it assumes all the load on its own threads.

- By convention, propeller diameter is marked first, then pitch.

- The colder and denser the water, the smaller a propeller should be. The rule, based on a starting temperature of 70 degrees F, is that the propeller diameter should be reduced about 1 percent for every 10 degree F drop in water temperature.

Pull, Maximum by One Person The maximum horizontal pull a person can exert on a line, given a good foothold, is about 150 pounds. When pulling downward, of course, maximum pull equals the weight of the person pulling.

See also: SWIGGING

Purchase, Calculation of, in Block and Tackle The purchase, or power, gained by a tackle, is equal to the number of lines leading into and away from the *moving block only*, including a line attached to its becket but excluding a line attached to the load.

Another way to say this is that the mechanical advantage of a tackle equals the number of parts pulling on the load. (A *part*, in this instance, means a line leading into or away from the sheave of the moving block or attached to the block's shell.)

Incidentally, a fixed block adds no power. It merely changes the direction of pull. When one tackle is applied to the hauling part of another, the total power gained is the power of the first multiplied by the power of the second.

Friction is traditionally reckoned at one-tenth of the load for every sheave the line passes over. In modern blocks with improved bearings, this figure might be excessive, but it gives an added safety factor in calculations.

P

127

R

Radar, Attention Span of Operators More than half of all vessel sightings are made in the first 30 minutes of radar watches lasting two hours or more.

A great deal of research has established that after the first half-hour, a radar operator's attention drops off considerably. If a yacht has radar aboard, and is relying on it in conditions of bad visibility, the watch should be relieved every 30 minutes if at all possible.

Radar, Changes in Direction In a collision situation, if you want your change of direction to be noticed on another vessel's radar screen, you must change course by at least 60 degrees.

Small changes of course are never easily discernible on a radar screen, even by experienced operators. To avoid collision, try to make a 60- to 90-degree change of course as early as possible.

Radar, Radiation from Check your radar manual for any reference to harmful radiation. If any doubt exists, keep the antenna above head level at all times while operating.

Radar Reflector, Efficiency of Reflective performance is proportional to the fourth power of linear dimension. In simpler terms, if you double the size, the effectiveness increases 16 times.

If we take a 12-inch reflector as standard, then a 15-inch reflector will have its effectiveness increased by about 250 percent. An 18-inch reflector is 500 percent better than a 12-inch. (This measurement is usually the diagonal measure quoted by yacht stores and manufacturers. Diagonals of 16 to 18 inches correspond to sides of about 11 to 13 inches.)

For peak efficiency, the reflector must be raised in *three-point suspension* or *raincatcher* attitude (with one of the eight pockets pointing straight up), not hung from a single corner.

It should be noted that most experienced small-boat sailors have little faith in radar reflectors. If you can imagine a highly focused spotlight on an approaching ship trying to receive a direct reflection of its own light from a mirror attached to your mast, you'll understand why.

Other, fancier kinds of radar reflectors present multiple facets to collect and return the transmission, or use the properties of concentric layers of plastic material to focus and return a beam. So far, nobody seems to be claiming 100-percent efficiency, either, although they have to be an improvement on the two-piece, slot-together, foil-covered cardboard affair that the skipper produces from under his or her mattress in times of panic.

R

129

Radio, Converting Frequency and Wavelength

The modern tendency is to name radio transmissions by their frequency, measured in cycles per second, rather than by their wavelength in meters, which was the method used extensively a few decades ago. A frequency of one cycle per second is what the scientist calls a hertz, named after the German physicist Heinrich Rudolph Hertz. One kilohertz (kHz) equals 1,000 cycles a second, and one megahertz (MHz) equals 1 million cycles a second.

But frequency and wavelength bear a fixed relation to each other and you can convert MHz into meters, or vice versa, by dividing into 300.

Radio, Transmission Distances Effective
range varies greatly, but the following are widely
accepted rules of thumb:

- VHF (Very High Frequency) is essentially line-of-sight, limited by antenna height.

- Range between boats is about 25 miles.

- Range between a boat and a land station can be up to 50 miles.

- Range between a boat and a high-flying aircraft can be up to 300 miles.

- Range from hand-held to hand-held stations is about 3 miles.

- SSB (Single Side-Band) radio ranges vary from as little as 50 miles on the 4 MHz band to as much as 10,000 miles on the 22 MHz band.

Radio Direction Finder, Emergency In a
pinch, you can use your local AM radio station to find
your way home at night or in fog.

Most portable radios with built-in ferrite rod
antennas are directionally sensitive and give a fairly
sharp null (little or no broadcast reception) when the
antenna is pointed end-on to the transmitter.
However, you should temper this knowledge with
common sense and caution, and make sure you
locate the transmitter correctly on your chart. Also,
be quite certain that you are tuned to *that* transmitter and not to a repeater or a siren sound-alike that
will lure you onto the rocks.

I once used this method to obtain a rough but welcome indication of the whereabouts of the island of
Barbados after obtaining doubtful sextant shots in
poor weather.

Incidentally, the cheaper the radio, the better it
works as a direction finder. Expensive radios have
better antennas and extra circuits to improve reception in the null zone, which is exactly what you *don't*
need.

Range Markers, Which One to Follow

Range markers, or transit marks, when lined up, guide you safely along a channel or into an anchorage.

Usually, one marker is higher than the other for better visibility, but unless you're used to following ranges it can be difficult to know which way to steer when the two markers fall out of line.

The rule of thumb is to follow the front (lower) one. If it appears to be drifting off to starboard of the back marker, you, too, should steer to starboard to get them lined up again and regain your proper course.

See also: CIRCLES OF POSITION

Red Right Returning

In U.S. waters, the rule of thumb for vessels returning to harbor from the sea is to leave red (nun) buoys on the vessel's right (starboard) side.

This is the International Association of Lighthouse Authorities' (IALA's) System B. Green (can) buoys mark the port side of the channel and should be left to port.

Nun buoys, incidentally, are conical, or pointed on top. Can buoys are flat on top. Numbers on red buoys normally are even. Numbers on green buoys are almost invariably odd.

However, in what seems almost a deliberate attempt to confuse the unwary amateur, lighted buoys, whether red or green, do not necessarily conform to the nun or can shapes. From a distance in daylight, most lighted buoys look like can buoys with their middles missing; but their silhouettes give no indication of what side of the channel they guard.

Red-and-green buoys with horizontal bands mark channel junctions or hazards that you may pass on either side while proceeding from the sea. Look for the color of the topmost band or, at night, the light. If it's green, then the preferred channel is the one you'll naturally enter if you leave the buoy to port of

R

131

your boat. If it's red, the preferred channel is gained by leaving the buoy to starboard.

In other words, red or green topmost bands lend the buoy the characteristics of the same color nun or can buoy, as far as the *preferred* channel is concerned. Incidentally, note that you might not be able to pass safely on either side of a junction buoy when *returning* to sea.

Red-and-white vertically striped buoys mark a fairway or midchannel. You may pass them on either side, but it's best to leave them to port if you can, as this correctly places you on the starboard side of the channel. These buoys also divide the channels in a Traffic Separation Scheme.

Reefing, When to Reef Here are three basic rules of thumb about the timing of reefing:

1. Reef before you have to.

2. When sailing downwind, reef as if you were sailing upwind.

3. When in doubt, take in a double reef.

Rule 1 simply indicates that it's easier to shorten sail before your vessel becomes totally overwhelmed by the wind.

Rule 2 is a reminder of how easy it is to misjudge the wind's speed while sailing a free course. Try to judge wind speed at all times—the real wind speed, not the apparent wind speed—and reef as if you were sailing to weather in the same strength wind.

Rule 3 is an acknowledgment of the fact that you can't always tell how much harder the wind will be blowing in 10 or 20 minutes. In a sudden squall, for example, it makes more sense to shorten sail more drastically than might be needed immediately, because it's usually a simpler matter to shake out a reef than to tuck one in.

When to reef? Before you lose control. On the wind, the signs are pretty obvious: excessive heel, sidedecks awash, lack of response to the helm, hardheadedness (griping), and overwhelming weather helm. Off the wind, watch for prolonged surfing and a sloppy, dead feeling to the helm as a wave passes underneath. Watch for rearing, threatening quarter waves, and a tendency for the bow to plunge headlong into the trough ahead. Time to slow down.

Another clever time to tuck in a double reef is before you drop the mainsail at an open roadstead or any anchorage where you might later find yourself caught on a lee shore.

If the wind comes blasting through at gale force in the middle of the night, you won't want to be messing around with raising a full mainsail and trying to reef it in the dark. You'll be wanting to get the hell out there under the nice snug, controllable rig you so cleverly arranged before you turned in.

Rigging, Running, Types of Line for

Either three-stranded Dacron or the more popular braided Dacron is recommended for all sheets. On cruising boats, Dacron can also be used for rope halyards provided it's pre-stretched and of the highest quality. Nylon should never be used for sheets or halyards.

Rigging, Standing, Size of Standard rules of thumb for cruising boats:

Shrouds: Total breaking strength of all shrouds on one side of the boat should equal about 1.2 times the vessel's displacement. Racing boats and daysailers: about 1.0 times displacement. Serious offshore cruisers: about 1.4 times displacement.

(If you have double lower shrouds, as most boats have, assume only one is working at any one time—in other words, use only one lower shroud for this calculation, and then make the other shroud the same dimension.)

Dividing the load between upper and lower shrouds: Single-spreader rig: Lower 60 percent, upper 40 percent.

Double-spreader rig: Lower 48 percent, intermediate 26 percent, upper 26 percent.

(Where intermediate and upper shrouds combine at the lower spreader and run to a single turnbuckle and chainplate, the combined intermediate/upper shroud should carry 52 percent of the load.)

Spreader locations: A single-spreader (or crosstree, as they're sometimes called) needs to be between 50 and 52 percent of the height from deck to masthead, measured from the deck upward. In a double-spreader rig, the lower spreader should be 37 to 39 percent of the way up the mast, and the upper spreader should be 68 to 70 percent of the way up.

Headstay: Should be the size of the heaviest shroud or one size larger.

Backstay: Same size as headstay.

Turnbuckles: For standard, open-body bronze turnbuckles the screw diameter should be twice the rigging wire diameter. (High-strength stainless steel turnbuckles can be a little lighter.)

Opening between the turnbuckle jaws: Twice the wire diameter.

Clevis pin: Twice the rigging wire diameter.

Rigging golden rule: Always insert toggles (universal joints) between turnbuckle and chainplate and between mast tang and shroud eye. This cuts down on metal fatigue and unexpected failure.

See also: APPENDIX: BREAKING STRENGTH OF 1 X 19 STAINLESS STEEL RIGGING WIRE

Rigging, Tautness of When on a beam reach under normal sail in a moderate breeze, the shrouds on the leeward side of a Bermuda-rigged yacht should *feel* slightly slack, but not *look* slack to the casual observer.

Right of Way Despite your having the right of way under the International or Inland Collision Regulations, you are required by law to give way if the other vessel fails to do so in time to prevent a collision. Common sense often dictates that you should give a wide berth to large ships when you have the right of way—but make your change of course a substantial one, and make it early, so that the give-way vessel understands your intentions. If having to give way when you're in the right irritates you, remember the old epitaph:

> *Here lies the body of Michael O'Day*
>
> *Who died maintaining his right of way.*
>
> *He was right, dead right, as he sailed along,*
>
> *But he's just as dead as if he'd been wrong.*

See also: RULES OF THE ROAD

Rising and Dipping of Lights

One of the quickest and easiest ways to fix your position is by noting when the light of a lighthouse rises above, or dips below the sea horizon.

You can find your distance away from a known lighthouse without plotting anything on the chart simply by using the Distance of Sea Horizon table in the Appendix. For a full fix, take these simple steps:

- •Take the bearing of the light when it is level with your horizon.

- •Use the Distance of Sea Horizon table to find the distance from your eye to the horizon. Use the table again to find the distance from the light to the horizon. These figures come from the height of your eye above sea level and the height of the lighthouse above sea level, which is given on the chart.

- •Add the two distances together.

- •Plot the bearing from the lighthouse on your chart and mark along it the total distance off.

Roller Furling, Reliability of

Roller furling and reefing works well for weekend sailors and coastal cruisers with ports close at hand. But short-handed ocean cruisers should view it with suspicion, because if anything should go wrong at sea it could result in a dangerous amount of canvas being set, or at least being left to flap aloft. Repairs at sea could be extremely difficult, if not impossible, without a large and skilled crew.

After years of cruising and dozens of delivery jobs, Lin Pardey said: "Larry and I figure we are now batting 1,000. We haven't yet delivered a boat with a roller furling jib that worked correctly in all situations."

Yes, it's true that round-the-world singlehanded racers use roller furling. But these are sailing's Supermen. They are no ordinary mortals. They hoist themselves up forestays in the Roaring Forties to slash their headsails free of stuck roller furlers and think nothing of it.

Manufacturers will tell you that their products have improved since the Pardeys gave their opinion on roller furling. Maybe. But remember this: Jibs with hanks always come down.

Rope, Braided, Coiling of To allow a braided line to render freely through a block or other constriction, the experts advocate coiling it with alternate hitch coiling.

Rigging expert Brion Toss explains in his book, *The Rigger's Apprentice*, that alternate coil hitching is a method of coiling whereby regular turns, which impart twists in one direction, are alternated with hitches that impart twists in the other direction.

These twists are said to cancel each other out and result in a kink-free line.

I'm almost ashamed to admit that I've never had any trouble with coils of braided line. I build in a little twist when I first coil them, as I would with a stranded line.

Then, when it's time to remove halyard coils from

their cleats, it's my practice to dump them on deck for a little free-style writhing, after which they seem pleased to render themselves through blocks or anything else without fuss.

If you have a long line that must run clear at high speed without snarls, lay it down on deck in the shape of figure eights, one on top of the other. I expect the experts know this as a double alternate horizontal coil hitch, but I'm not sure.

Rope, Braided, Splicing of

The rule about whether or not you should learn to splice braided line is quite simple. If you don't learn, you'll be confronted with a desperate need for splices everywhere you look. If you do go to the trouble of learning, you'll never find a need for a splice again.

Many sailors capable of tying a bowline see no need for an eye-splice in braided line. It looks complicated, and needs special equipment.

But in fact the equipment is cheap and lasts as long as anything else on a boat, which is to say until it rusts or falls overboard.

In any case, any sailor worth his or her salt should know how to do it. All-rope halyards made from braided line *need* eye-splices because splices weaken a line less than do knots. All in all, I'm definitely in favor of learning to splice braided line. Maybe next year.

Rope, Three-Stranded, Coiling of

If the rope you're trying to coil is writhing and squirming like a cobra in mating season, chances are you're coiling a three-stranded line the wrong way.

Nearly all the three-stranded line you're likely to come across on pleasure boats is laid up right-handed—that is, if you look at a piece of rope going away from you, the strands twist to the right, or clockwise. It likes to be coiled that way, too, and (like the cobra) does not take kindly to being thwarted.

Rope, Turning into Line
Although you buy rope as rope, it mysteriously turns into line the moment you get it aboard your boat.

When you apply it to many specific uses, the line then assumes the name of the rigging part it has become. There are very few ropes on a boat, apart from a bolt rope, a tiller rope, a foot rope, and a few others now rarely used.

Instead, your new rope may turn into a sheet, a halyard, a warp, a rode, a pendant, a painter, a hawser, a strop, a cable, a mooring line, a dock line, a leech line, a heaving line, a downhaul, an outhaul, an uphaul, a guy, reef points, a lashing, a lanyard, a kicking strap, a preventer, a vang, or even a fender around the tender.

Rope, Working Strength of
Safety experts say their rule of thumb for the working load of three-strand laid line is that it not exceed 11 percent of its tensile strength.

Now this is one of those statistics that gnaws at the mind. Why not a nice round figure like 10 percent? Or 25 percent? Eleven percent, besides being a very odd figure, also seems awfully low. That's using only about one-tenth of the line's ultimate strength, which might seem to some to be an expensive and wasteful way to go about things.

Braided rope, on the other hand, may be pressed into use at 20 percent of its breaking strength. They say the core of braided rope is better protected as it ages. But in figuring this out for themselves, boaters should be encouraged to combine common sense with frequent inspection.

I must say that 25 percent seems to be a perfectly reasonable figure for three-strand rope—with the possible exception of the anchor rode and the halyard that's hauling me up the mast in the bosun's chair.

Ropes, Stretch Rates of
At 30 percent of breaking load:

- Nylon stretches about 10 to 15 percent.
- Dacron (Terylene) stretches about 3.5 to 5 percent.
- Wire rope (stainless, 7 x 19) stretches about 1 to 2 percent.
- Kevlar and Spectra stretch about 1 to 2 percent.

Ropes, Various Materials and Their Uses

The three most commonly encountered synthetic materials used to make boating ropes are nylon, polyester, and polypropylene. Their uses are:

Nylon: For mooring, towing, and anchor lines, where its great strength and ability to stretch is an advantage.

Polyester (Dacron, Terylene, Duron, Fortrel, A.C.E., and Kodel are trademarks): For sheets and halyards, where excessive stretch would be detrimental.

Polypropylene: For heaving lines and dinghy painters. It's comparatively cheap and it floats, but it's more affected by sunlight, has little elasticity, and tends not to retain knots.

Other newer synthetic fibers—such as Kevlar and Spectra, which combine great strength with very little stretch—are still comparatively expensive and mostly used aboard serious racing yachts.

R

139

Rudder, Efficiency of

A narrow, deep rudder is more efficient than a broad, shallow rudder. The farther aft the rudder is placed, the greater its turning leverage.

For powerboats and racing sailboats, a balanced rudder with about 17 percent of the area forward of the pivoting axis provides a lighter helm and quicker response.

For cruising sailboats, an unbalanced rudder hung from a skeg or a full keel benefits from a smoother flow of water, and offers less resistance.

Rudder, Stall Angle of Ordinary rudders are most effective when angled at 35 degrees to the flow of water. The often-succumbed-to temptation to exceed this angle results only in a stall and unnecessary strain from excessive water pressure.

I have noticed, in fin-keel sailboats especially, that you can with benefit put the helm farther over than 35 degrees after the stern has started to swing—but that still doesn't mean the angle of incidence between the rudder and the water is any greater than 35 degrees.

Rudder Stock, Sailboat The traditional formula for calculating the size of solid bronze rudder stocks on sailboat rudders supported at the top is: Stock diameter in inches equals 0.16 times the waterline beam in feet. Stainless-steel stocks can be proportionately thinner.

See also: APPENDIX: TENSILE STRENGTH OF MATERIALS USED IN BOATBUILDING

Rule of Thumb, the Original *See*: DANGERS, KEEPING CLEAR OF

Rules of the Road Who gives way to whom? In this list, under normal circumstances a vessel gives way to every other vessel listed before it. But see the three exceptions noted below:

- A vessel not under command
- A vessel restricted in her ability to maneuver
- A vessel constrained by her draft
- A vessel engaged in fishing
- A sailing vessel
- A power-driven vessel

Be aware that a vessel not under command (unable, through *exceptional* circumstances, to maneuver to keep clear of another vessel) *must* show the correct signal: two balls or similar shapes in a vertical line, or two all-round red lights in a vertical line.

Similarly, a vessel that, from the nature of her work, is restricted in her ability to maneuver (except for a minesweeper) *must* exhibit a ball, a diamond, and a ball in a vertical line, or a red light, white light, and red light in a vertical line.

A vessel constrained by her draft *may* show three all-round red lights in a vertical row, or a cylinder (with the axis vertical). If she has any sense, she *will*.

Exceptions to the give-way list above:

- Rule 9 says a vessel of less than 20 meters (66 feet) in length, or a sailing vessel of any length, must keep clear of any vessel that can navigate safely only within a *narrow channel or fairway*.

- Rule 10 says a vessel less than 66 feet in length, or a sailing vessel of any size, shall not impede the passage of a power-driven vessel following a traffic lane in a traffic separation scheme.

- Rule 13 is another overriding rule. It says the overtaking vessel shall keep clear. Always. If a speedy sailboat overtakes a sluggish powerboat of any size, the sailboat must keep clear.

R

141

And if you are overtaking in a narrow channel, you must always correctly signal your intention to overtake, and receive acknowledgment, if you're in a powerboat. In a sailboat, you may overtake without signaling, but only under the Inland Rules.

See also: SOUND SIGNALS, WHEN TO MAKE THEM; AND APPENDIX: SOUND SIGNALS, MOST COMMON

Rum Punch, Caribbean, Recipe for   The traditional recipe for Caribbean rum punch is "One of sour, two of sweet, three of strong, and four of weak."

It was never for the faint of heart. Planter's Punch

consists of the juice of one lime or lemon, two heaped teaspoons of sugar, three ounces of best Jamaica rum, and four ounces of dry gin.

Running Aground, First Action to Take

In a sailboat, your first reaction on running aground should be to try to spin the boat about to face deep water. In a powerboat, it might make more sense to keep the propellers in deeper water and apply full power astern.

The two basic methods of refloating a sailboat are to use force to drag her into deeper water (with the aid of another boat, or by using anchors and winches) or to reduce her draft by heeling her, lightening her, or both. Either method is much easier if she is facing deep water.

Running an Inlet Here is age-old advice for those thinking of crossing a strange bar for the first time in heavy onshore winds: Don't. You'll be safer riding out the gale at sea. The ancient rule of thumb is: When in doubt, stay out.

However, if for some reason you positively have to run an inlet, here are some tips that *might* help save your life:

- Call ashore for advice. Try Channel 16 on your VHF, or use a cellular telephone.

If this brings no success, proceed thus:

- Have a good long look from seaward for the lowest surf, which indicates the deepest water over the bar. Approach the surf line with great caution. It never looks as bad from seaward as it really is.

- Wait, if you can, until the flood tide is flowing into the inlet.

- Look for a pattern to the swells. Often the third or fifth or seventh wave is bigger. That's not a fairy tale. It happens when complex but regular swell patterns ride on each other's backs.

- Stand off until a big swell has broken and then run in behind it. Try to stay slightly forward of the bottom of the trough, matching your speed to the swells and keeping them dead ahead and astern.

- Keep a sharp watch on what's happening to the waves behind you as well as those in front of you.

- Say your prayers.

R

S

Sail Area, Average To estimate the necessary sail area, take three-quarters of the square of the waterline length in feet—that is, multiply the waterline length by itself and take 75 percent of the result. The answer is in square feet.

Sail Area, Cruising About 85 square feet of working sail area for every 2,000 pounds of displacement produces a boat that is a nimble and efficient passagemaker in light to medium winds.

"Do not, no matter what your instincts are, cut down the size or height of your rig to go voyaging," warn Lin and Larry Pardey. "Cruising boats need power to keep them moving, since they are almost always heavily laden."

Sail Area, Maximum for One Person A sail of about 400 square feet is about as much as one person working alone would want to handle with any regularity. The British designer-sailor Uffa Fox held that one man could "reef or stow a 500-square-foot mainsail in all weathers." But he was an exceptional sailor. Sir Francis Chichester, on the other hand, decided that his mainsail of 380 square feet was more than he could manage in heavy weather.

Often the size and seakeeping qualities of the hull come into play here. It's not unreasonable to speculate that a larger hull, providing a more stable working platform, might ease the handling of a larger sail.

Sail Area, Running Downwind The cruiser's rule of thumb is never to run downwind with more sail than you would be carrying in the same breeze upwind. Of course, racers carry downwind all the sail they are able to, and sometimes more.

Sail Area/Displacement Ratio This is a measure of a sailboat's power compared to its weight. It's calculated as sail area in square feet (or meters) divided by displacement in cubic feet (or cubic meters) to the two-thirds power.

Here are the accepted SA/DISP ratios for different kinds of boats:

Cruising boats:	16 to 18
Cruiser/racers:	18 to 20
Racers:	20 to 22
High-performance racers:	22+
Racing multihulls:	28+

Sail Cloth, Weight of For everyday working sails, main and fore, divide the waterline length of the boat by 3. The answer is in ounces of cloth per square yard.

Sailmaker's Palm, Care of A sailmaker's palm is a valuable tool aboard any sailboat that indulges in voyaging or frequent passagemaking. You'll never know how valuable it is until you really need it. Like a sextant, a good one should last you a lifetime, and the rule of thumb is that you should keep the leather supple by rubbing in some Neatsfoot oil every six months or so.

Salt, Spilled The ancient rule, at sea as well as on land, is that a pinch of spilled salt should be tossed over the shoulder, otherwise misfortune will follow.

It does not seem to matter which shoulder you toss it over. If you're right-handed, it's somewhat easier to toss it over your left shoulder; and it's perhaps a little more difficult and ceremonial to toss it over your right. I'm a right-hander and I prefer to use the right shoulder, because the more trouble you to appease the gods, the better they like it.

Salvage Claims
In general, three conditions must be fulfilled for a salvage claim to be valid:

- The vessel must have been in genuine distress—that is, in danger of being damaged or destroyed, in the judgment of its owner.

- The person offering help must do so voluntarily.

- The salvage effort must be successful.

By law and by custom, mariners are required to save lives at sea. However, there is no such obligation to save the vessel. Thus, anyone saving a vessel in distress may qualify as a salvor and be entitled to an award.

To avoid salvage claims, ask your potential rescuer (before you pass or accept any lines) whether there will be a charge for the service. If there is, and you agree on a price, the salvor becomes a contractor and may not claim salvage.

You cannot be forced to accept a tow to safety, no matter how desperate the situation is, but there may come a time when it is your last resort. If you accept help in the absence of any agreement on price, and a valid salvage effort is undertaken, your rescuer may qualify for a claim.

Your ability to help yourself and the contribution you make to your own salvation may lessen the amount of any award to your salvor. Don't abandon your boat if it's not necessary. Don't accept his towline if you have one that is suitable. Give him yours. The less you rely on his special skills, abilities, equipment, and knowledge, the weaker will be his claim in Admiralty Court. Remember, a salvage award is usually based on the amount by which the salvor's efforts improved the situation—and this amount has to be significant.

Schooner Masts, Names of There aren't many seven-masted schooners around any longer. However, if you should come across one, it would be very satisfying to be able to name all her masts.

From the bow, aft:

Two masts:	Fore and main
Three masts:	Fore, main, and spanker
Four masts:	Fore, main, mizzen, and spanker
Five masts:	Fore, main, mizzen, jigger, and spanker
Six masts:	Fore, main, mizzen, jigger, driver, and spanker
Seven masts:	Fore, main, mizzen, jigger, driver, pusher, and spanker

Screws, Dimensions for Use in Wood The old rule of thumb used by builders of wooden boats was that a screw needed to have a thread depth of at least six times its shank diameter near the head to obtain its maximum grip in hardwood. For softwood, that ratio was increased to 8:1.

Sculling Notch, Dinghy The usual size for a sculling notch in the transom of a work dinghy or yacht tender is 1⅛ inches wide by 2½ inches deep. It could, with benefit, be slightly narrower at the top than the bottom and all edges should be well rounded.

Scurvy, Incidence of Despite the abundance of vitamin pills, symptoms of scurvy still often manifest themselves among long-distance sailors. Scurvy is characterized by weakness, anemia, spongy gums, and bleeding from mucous membranes.

Vitamin C, as found in fresh foodstuffs, is the best preventive, but boats without refrigeration are handicapped in this respect. Excellent sources of nutrition that keep well are cabbage, carrots, celery, winter squash, garlic, grapefruit, lemons (perhaps the all-round best anti-scorbutic), onions, potatoes, oranges, and green fruit or vegetables that will ripen on the voyage, such as apples, bananas, and tomatoes.

Dr. Hannes Lindemann—who made two Atlantic crossings, one in a dug-out canoe and one in a rubber-and-canvas folding boat—strongly recommends raw onions for the prevention of scurvy, and says garlic is useful.

Incidentally, this unusually perceptive adventurer also thinks it very important that voyagers carry beer, among other things, for calories and energy.

Seacocks Every underwater hole through a boat's hull should be fitted with a reliable seacock.

It's a simple and obvious safety rule, but it's surprising how many boats don't have seacocks. What a seacock provides is a quick, positive way to prevent the sea coming in through that hole when you don't want it to.

There are three basic types of seacocks: the bronze, tapered plug type; the bronze gate valve type, and the glass-reinforced nylon Marelon or "plastic" type with a ball valve.

I personally prefer the tapered plug because when it seizes, as any seacock will if it's not opened and shut fairly frequently, it can easily be freed by light taps with a hammer. I have done this quickly, easily, and without danger in mid-ocean while in the process of dismantling a blocked toilet.

Seized plastic seacocks have sometimes failed when force was applied to the handle and the torque broke the operating spindle. This problem has been addressed by manufacturers and should no longer be a problem. Marelon is very strong, corrosion free, light, and cheaper than a bronze tapered plug.

Gate valves don't make very satisfactory seacocks because you can't tell at a glance whether they're open, shut, or halfway in between. Sometimes, when you think you've screwed them down tight, they're actually still partially open because they've clamped down on a piece of debris. You can't through-bolt them to the hull in the approved fashion, either, because they have no flanges. All in all, not the best choice.

Seakindliness, Definition of Howard I. Chapelle defined seakindliness as "the ability of a boat to meet heavy weather and remain reasonably dry, shipping no solid water and relatively little spray."

Interestingly, this eminent naval architect was of the opinion that few boats under 40 feet in length could meet the other requirements of seakindliness, namely, that they should permit comfort for the crew through a slow easy roll (with no jerk or sudden stop at the end of each one) and an equally slow and easy pitch.

Chapelle asserted that if a boat under 40 feet were to be safe in heavy weather, the very characteristics of the quick motion required to prevent her from shipping solid water would make her uncomfortable for her crew, to the extent that it would be impossible to stand or walk without clinging to supports. It's scant consolation while it's happening, but reassuring nevertheless to know that such diabolical motion is deliberately designed into the boat, and is necessary if she is to survive severe weather.

See also: SEAWORTHINESS, DEFINITION OF

Seamanship, the Highest Order of The most professional sailors are those who know what to do after things have gone wrong.

Truly competent boaters are always asking themselves, "What if...?" What if the engine failed in this narrow harbor entrance? What if the wind switched 180 degrees and the anchor started dragging toward land? What if a fuel tank sprang a leak? Knowing what to do—having a plan, no matter how sketchy—

S

149

makes the difference between competence and incompetence. Good sailors bring their ships home safely even after things have gone wrong.

Seamanship, Where It Starts Good seamanship starts in port. It may sound trite, but it's a rule that's as true now as it was centuries ago. Detailed preparation is the secret to a successful passage. Careful checking of all running and standing gear and the diligent compilation of commissioning lists count as much toward seamanship as the physical skills born of long experience.

See also: BLACK BOX THEORY, VIGOR'S

Seasickness, Adaptation to Anyone who has avoided seasickness during the first three days of a cruise usually has adapted to the motion and is unlikely to get seasick later during that same trip.

The after-effects of adaptation (swaying ground, rocking bed, and so forth) can be felt for two or three days after a voyage. Once having adapted, a person is immune to seasickness for 6 to 10 weeks. No re-adaptation will be needed for subsequent cruises starting during that period.

Note: A sick crewmember should never be allowed to hang over the rail. It's dangerous. Use a bucket or bowl. Or have brown paper bags available, and throw the bags overboard.

The most suitable work for sick crew is steering or lookout duty.

Seasickness, Prevention of The golden rules are to stay away from alcohol, greasy foods, and engine-room smells; keep warm and dry, stay on deck, keep busy if possible, and watch the horizon.

To which may be added: Take medications *before* sailing or the occurrence of rough weather. The general rule is to take them three hours before. If you wait until you start to feel sick, it's too late for the medicine's prophylactic properties to take effect. Ginger, in soft drinks or cookies, may help prevent sickness. Stay away from the extreme ends of the boat where motion is worst.

Check with your doctor for allergies if you wish to try a new drug. Different drugs are effective for different people. Try a drug on land first to see what its side-effects are, but don't drive a car until you're sure it doesn't affect your ability.

Seasickness occurs less frequently when you lie down. The second most favorable position is standing upright, legs slightly apart, without holding on to anything—provided, of course, you're in no danger of going overboard. The position most conducive to seasickness is sitting down.

Seasickness, Susceptibility to Women become seasick more frequently than men.

Surveys indicate women are more susceptible to motion sickness; thus it takes less motion to make them nauseated. Infants and elderly people are less susceptible than others. Within the first three days of an Atlantic crossing on a large ship, between 25 and 30 percent of the passengers will be sick. On small yachts the percentage is higher. About 60 percent of people get sick in a small inflatable liferaft.

Seasickness, Symptoms of The symptoms of seasickness often occur in the following order: frequent yawning, slight headache, dry mouth, pallor, cold sweat, nausea, and sickness.

Seawater, Composition of The mineral content of seawater is about 3.5 percent. Common salt (sodium chloride) accounts for 78 percent of this, and magnesium chloride 11 percent. The other 11 percent is a mixture of a dozen or more minerals.

See also: OCEAN, MAIN CONSTITUENTS OF; AND OCEAN, SALTS PRESENT IN

Seawater, Drinking by Castaways The consensus of doctors having experience with castaways is that seawater should not be drunk except to augment an ample supply of fresh water, in which case as much as one pint of seawater a day might be acceptable.

John Voss drank a glass of seawater a day for his health, and I have drunk a small cupful of the South Atlantic every day for 30 days in a row without apparent ill effect. Sir Francis Chichester found that the occasional drink of seawater relieved leg cramps apparently caused by excessive sweating and salt loss in the tropics. But all of us were drinking plenty of fresh water as well.

Incidentally, if fresh water is scarce, the old rule is to cut down on food consumption also. Large amounts of water are needed to digest proteins, in particular.

Seawater, Drinking During Seasickness

Prolonged seasickness may cause a serious chemical imbalance in the human body. Small quantities of seawater, however, provide all the sodium and other chemicals needed to restore that balance, with the exception of calcium.

An eminent Cape Town sailor and physician, Dr. "Bags" Baigrie, once advised me to try to drink half a cup of sea water once or twice a day during prolonged bouts of seasickness. Although it was not likely to remain in the stomach long, he said, the tissues would swiftly absorb the minerals needed. He pointed out that salt water and human blood were very similar in chemical makeup.

Seaworthiness, Definition of

Here is Howard I. Chapelle's classic definition in *Yacht Designing and Planning*:

> *Seaworthiness is basically the ability of a boat to live in heavy weather without swamping, capsizing, breaking up or being heavily damaged while underway.*

She, as a Nautical Pronoun

There is a growing tendency, perhaps created by lubberly ignorance or possibly well-meant consideration for female sensitivities, to refer to a vessel as *it* rather than *she*. This seems erroneous and unnecessary.

Surely the issue here is one of semantics, not of disrespect toward women. Consider the French word *table*. A table is feminine, not because it has attractive legs but for grammatical reasons. English, though to a much lesser degree than French, also has words that are feminine in grammar but neuter in real life. For example, the correct pronoun for motherland is *it*. Why should the correct pronoun for a neuter ship not be *she*?

It's worth noting that women singlehanders with extensive experience in lone voyaging—such as Nicolette Milnes Walker, third woman to sail solo across the North Atlantic—invariably refer to their boats as *she* and *her* in speech and print.

More authoritatively, the International Regulations for Preventing Collisions at Sea—subscribed to by all the maritime nations of the world—and the Inland Rules of the United States, refer to ships as *she* and *her*.

Sheets, Headsail and Mainsail, Diameter of

The size of a sheet for a jib, a forestaysail, or a mainsail obviously depends on the size of the sail.

You can make a rough estimate of the strain on a jib sheet by squaring the wind speed in knots and multiplying the answer by the sail area in square feet. Divide the result by 232 and you have the approximate pull on the sheet in pounds.

Thus, a 200-square-foot jib in a 20-knot breeze generates a pull of about 345 pounds. The *maximum* pull the sail is likely to exert can be about double this figure.

Now, the working load for a Dacron line is 11 percent of the breaking strain, so you'd need a $\frac{7}{16}$-inch-diameter Dacron sheet (breaking strain is 3,500 pounds).

For 300 square feet of sail in that same 20-knot breeze, you'd need a $\frac{1}{2}$-inch Dacron sheet; for 400 square feet, a ⅝-inch sheet; and for 500 square feet, a ¾-inch sheet.

Quite obviously, these are conservative figures, and there are enormous reserves of strength in sheets of these sizes. In fact, you'll often see smaller sizes used. However, for long life, safety, and the weakening effect of knots, it's better to err on the generous side.

Incidentally, headsail and mainsail sheets are rarely less than ½ inch in diameter because anything thinner is not comfortable to trim by hand.

Mainsail sheets led to the middle of the boom should be about the same size as the headsail sheets, sail area for sail area. For multipart mainsail sheets led to the end of the boom, ½-inch-diameter Dacron is appropriate for all sail areas up to 500 square feet.

Ships, Large, Stopping Distance of A large ship moving at cruising speed needs a mile or more to stop or complete a turn.

Some vessels, including Very Large Crude Carriers (VLCCs), need considerably more. That's why it often makes sense for a pleasure boat to give way, even if she has the right of way. Make an easily identified, substantial change of course. And make it good and early.

Singlehanded Boats, Seaworthiness of

The most important characteristic concerning the seaworthiness of a boat intended to be singlehanded on long voyages is that she be capable of looking after herself in bad weather.

This being so, the primary requirement is that a monohull cruiser have a large range of stability— that is, through 130 degrees or more from dead upright. This is because a singlehander might often need to lie ahull in heavy weather. Such a range of stability comes from ample, low, keel ballast; reasonably heavy displacement; and narrow to moderate beam.

Singlehanded Boats, Size of
How large a boat can a singlehander manage? It's a question that's often asked, but it's rather like asking: How long is a piece of string? The answer is that it all depends.

It depends on the singlehander's physical fitness, strength, experience, nautical cunning, and determination.

However, there are two definite limiting factors that can help you decide how big a boat *you* might be able to handle with safety and confidence.

The first is the anchor. Can you raise the heaviest anchor on board without the help of a winch and get it onto the foredeck? In ordinary circumstances you wouldn't have to do this, but it's still a good indication of your strength and ability.

The second is whether you can reef (and lower, smother, and get gaskets around) the largest sail on board in all kinds of weather.

If you feel quite confident in your ability to manage these two things, you're probably physically able to singlehand that particular boat. There are many other factors to take into account, of course, not the least of which is your mental ability to withstand solitude and the often frightening prospect of having nobody but yourself to rely on.

Exceptionally skilled sailors are singlehandedly racing around the world in boats of 50 feet and more these days, but the average sailor would probably be wise to build up experience on boats of no more than 40 feet overall.

S

155

Singlehanded Voyagers, Motivation of
What compels an otherwise sane and reasonable sailor to set off alone across an ocean, or around the world? Here are 10 reasons proposed by Richard Henderson, a sailor and author with a profound knowledge of the singlehanded psyche:

Practical purposes: To test a theory, perhaps, or

to gather research material for a book or a study, to earn money, or win a race. Sometimes, because the boat isn't big enough for two.

Self-significance: To find one's place in the pecking order and acquire a sense of belonging.

Curiosity and fulfillment: A desire to see and experience things for oneself.

Recognition: This is allied to self-significance, but takes things a stage further and involves a desire for fame.

Independence: The need for the greatest possible freedom and control over one's own destiny.

Escapism: Closely allied to independence. A rebellion against routine and flight from personal and societal problems.

Adventurousness: Pandering to the restless spirit, the desire for novelty, travel, and excitement.

Competitiveness: This takes many forms, including personal competition with the ocean and one's inner fears, as well as the desire to win races or set records.

Solitude: Some introverts like being alone. Other people experience a spiritual cleansing that makes them more appreciative of subsequent human company.

Mother Sea: All life came from the sea. Some deep instinct, some unsummoned fascination, draws many people back.

Henderson comments, "It seems safe to say that all singlehanders possess at least some of these motivations in various combinations."

Size, According to Age How big a boat do you need? This old rule of thumb seems to make as much sense as any: She should be a foot on the waterline for every year of your age.

However, it's not a rule that should be carried to

extremes. You should add your own personal cut-off rule at, say, 35 or 40 and not feel obliged to own an overwhelming 100-footer when you reach your doddery century.

Size, Down Below The most reliable indicator of the amount of living room aboard any boat is displacement—that is, the actual weight of the boat loaded and ready for sea. Length overall, or length on deck, is not of itself an accurate basis for comparison.

A good rule of thumb for the displacement needed for safety and comfort is: Total weight of crew, stores, water, fuel, and personal gear multiplied by 7.5.

See also: WEIGHT, CREW AND STORES, ESTIMATES OF

Skid Fin, Size and Placing of Long, shallow power vessels and high-speed planing boats sometimes gain steering maneuverability from a small skeg or skid fin up forward. When one is called for, it should be located between 10 and 15 percent of the boat's overall length forward of her center of gravity (CG). The usual situation of the CG in a high-speed planing hull is about 60 percent of the waterline length aft of the bow. The area of the skid fin should be about 90 percent of the total rudder area.

S

157

Sound Signals, When to Make Them Most boaters know it's obligatory to make sound signals in fog. But you're also required to make them in snow, rain, dust storms or any other situation that results in what the rules call "restricted visibility," by day or by night.

Furthermore, you must make the signals when you're *near* an area of restricted visibility, even if you happen to be in brilliant sunshine yourself.

The point is to inform a large ship barreling along in a fog bank just half a mile away that you'll be right in her path when she pops out of it.

She'll have you on radar, you say? Don't ever count on it.

See also: APPENDIX: SOUND SIGNALS, MOST COMMON

Sound, Speed of, in Water and Air Sound travels through water more than four times faster than it travels through air.

In case you ever need to know, the figure for sound in water is about 4,800 feet a second. Could be useful if you wish to repair your depth sounder or communicate with a dolphin.

In air of 32 degrees F, at sea level, the speed of sound is 1,088 feet per second. In the sort of round figures a sailor appreciates, it takes sound roughly five seconds to travel a mile.

See also: ECHO PILOTAGE

Soundings, Definition of A boat is said to be *on-soundings* when she is within the 100-fathom line. In water deeper than 100 fathoms, it was inconvenient in bygone days to sound with a lead-line. Consequently, when a ship sailed out to sea beyond the 100-fathom line, she was said to be *off-soundings*.

Speed, Average at Sea Under sail, during an ocean crossing in a traditional cruising monohull, plan on averaging 100 miles in 24 hours.

This a conservative rule. Many yachts beat this distance easily, but for planning and victualing purposes it has proved its worth.

Speed, Definitions of The speed of vessels on salt water is measured in knots. The knot is defined as one nautical mile per hour. It is therefore redundant to say knots *per hour*. However, the correct term for vessels operating on most inland bodies of fresh water is *miles per hour*, meaning statute, or land, miles.

See also: MILES, DEFINITIONS OF

Speed, Estimating A rough idea of a boat's speed can be had by noting the time in seconds that it takes to travel its own hull length.

The first thing you need to do is multiply the length of your boat, in feet, by 0.59. Keep the answer handy. You can use it foreverafter.

The next thing you need to do is throw a piece of orange peel overboard at the bow, and note the time in seconds it takes to reach the stern.

Now take the first number and divide it by the second. The answer is your speed in knots.

Speed can also be judged—especially the speed of a boat alongside—by the number of waves formed on the windward side between the bow and the stern.

A displacement hull making full hull speed lies in the trough of one large wave of her own making. The speed in knots of the boat at that stage is 1.34 times the square root of her waterline length in feet.

At half hull speed, she forms two waves on her windward side, at one-third hull speed she forms three waves, and so on. Count the number of waves, divide that number into the theoretical maximum hull speed, and you have a pretty accurate idea of her speed.

S

Speed, Knots in Yards/Minute As near as dammit:

1 knot = 33 yards a minute

2 knots = 66 yards a minute

3 knots = 100 yards a minute

4 knots = 130 yards a minute

5 knots = 165 yards a minute

6 knots = *Exactly* 1 nautical mile every 10 minutes

A boat's speed in knots also equals the number of hundred yards it travels in three minutes. Savvy powerboat navigators use these facts to great advantage. The rest of us just hope they'll come in useful some day.

Speed, Maximum, Displacement Hulls
The speed of non-planing hulls, whether under power or sail, is governed principally by waterline length. The formula for determining maximum speed is: Hull speed, in knots, equals 1.34 times the square root of the waterline length in feet. Or, hull speed, in knots, equals 3.28 times the square root of the waterline length in meters.

Speed, Maximum, Planing Hulls
The speed of a planing hull is determined mostly by the amount of power available. The most critical factor is the power-to-weight ratio.

An average planing hull can achieve speeds in the region of 25 knots if there is about 40 pounds of weight—boat, crew, fuel, stores, everything—for every unit of horsepower delivered to the propeller.

For that speed to increase to 50 knots, the weight per horsepower has to drop to about 10 pounds.

Obviously, this is self-limiting because the bigger and more powerful the engine, the more it weighs and the more fuel it consumes.

Speed, Maximum, Semi-Planing Hulls
The maximum speed of a semi-planing, or semi-displacement, hull depends on how closely related it is to one or the other. Usually, it's a bit faster than a full-displacement hull and not nearly as fast as a full-planing hull.

I've always been puzzled by semi-displacement hulls. I've always felt that displacement, or planing, was absolute, like pregnancy. Just as no one can be half pregnant, so no boat can be semi-displacement.

However, there does exist a hull shape that gets some of its lift from the dynamic action of the water passing beneath its hull at speed, and some from the hull's natural buoyancy.

This unnatural creature is plainly the designer's

answer to calls for more speed from the owners of full-displacement powercruisers tired of "crawling" around at eight knots.

The result, as usual, is an uncomfortable compromise that calls for a great increase in power and delivers a very modest increase in speed. Speed, in fact, is gained in a cumbersome fashion at the price of ultimate seaworthiness, carrying capacity, fuel consumption, or all three.

The semi-displacement hull, often with rounded sections forward, flattening out into a planing surface aft, labors mightily to break out of the deep wave it digs for itself.

It succeeds partially, but can never pop up onto a full, flat plane and start flying over the water like its planing brother.

Speed Trials, Rules for When conducting speed trials on a measured-mile course, remember these rules:

- The water must be reasonably deep. Shallow water creates a sinking action that holds a boat back.

- Time the boat in seconds going one way over the course.

- The speed equals 3,600 divided by the number of seconds.

- Time the boat in seconds going the opposite way over the course.

- Find the speed, as before, and then average the two speeds to find the true speed through the water.

- Do not average the two times, as this gives an incorrect result.

- If the measured mile is a statute mile of 5,280 feet, the result is in miles per hour. If it's a nautical mile of 6,076 (formerly 6,080) feet, the speed is in knots.

Spreaders, Angle of Spreaders should be higher at their tips than at their point of attachment to the mast. This not only looks more pleasing, it is also structurally stronger.

A spreader should exactly bisect the angle formed by the topmast shroud as it passes from deck level, around the spreader tip and on up to the masthead. In other words, the angle formed between the spreader and that part of the shroud leading upward should exactly equal the angle between the spreader and that part of the shroud leading downward. If this puzzles you, draw a diagram. It's important.

Stability in Powerboats, as Shown by Roll Time

A reliable rule of thumb is that a powerboat should have a roll time in seconds equal to between 1 and 1.1 times her overall beam in meters—that is, her overall beam in feet divided by 3.28. (Where waterline beam is less than 90 percent of overall beam, as in a boat with a large amount of flare, overall beam should be reckoned as waterline beam plus 11 percent.) This ensures the best compromise between stiffness and comfort. Boats with much shorter roll times have great initial stability, but probably have an uncomfortably jerky motion at sea. Boats with much longer roll times have less stability and should be handled with greater care when off-soundings.

Roll time can be ascertained fairly accurately on a calm day at the dock. A sufficiency of people should press down on the gunwale in unison until she is rolling as hard as she can. All hands should cease pushing when she is at the bottom of her roll toward the dock. With a stopwatch, time her roll from this position *back* to this position (or as near as she comes), to the nearest tenth of a second. If she's 10 feet wide, roll time should be in the region of 3 seconds. Repeat several times and take an average.

Stability in Sailboats, as Shown by Roll
Time Roll timing (see above) is usually not quite such an accurate indication of stability for ballasted monohull sailboats because of the inertia of the mast and the resistance of the keel and skegs. However, the following rough figures should either reassure you or scare you sufficiently to seek further advice. The figures given are roll times in seconds multiplied by *beam overall measured in meters*:

- Heavy displacement cruisers, 25 percent or less ballast ratio, no high deckhouse or cabintop: 0.95

- Heavy cruisers, 25 to 35 percent ballast ratio, nothing unusual on deck: 0.90

- Medium cruisers, 35 percent or more ballast, no high cabins: 0.85

- Cruiser/racers, 35 percent or more ballast, moderate draft and moderate cabin height: 0.80

- Racers, 40 percent ballast or more, deep draft, low cabintops: 0.75

- Fringe racers, 45+ percent ballast ratio, extra deep keels: 0.70

S

Stainless Steel, Corrosion of It seems almost paradoxical, but most types of stainless steel rely on a constant supply of oxygen to avoid corrosion. On deck, or under water, uncovered stainless steel receives sufficient oxygen and stays bright. But if it's enclosed in a stern tube, covered with marine growth or surrounded by wood, stagnant water, or other material, it can be deprived of oxygen and suffer severely from pitting. That's one good reason why the stern gland should drip a little—to feed oxygen to the stainless steel propeller shaft—and that's why it isn't always clever to use stainless steel for keel bolts.

According to well-known marine author Nigel

163

Calder, stainless steel is an alloy of several metals, one of which is chromium.

When the chromium is exposed to oxygen, in air or water, it forms an inert layer that protects the underlying metal.

"But if taken away from oxygen and surrounded by moisture, particularly salt water, the oxidized layer of chromium breaks down, leaving the stainless steel to rust and corrode much like ordinary steel—a situation commonly referred to as *crevice corrosion*," said Calder in an article in the September/October 1992 issue of *Ocean Navigator*.

The prudent mariner should look with suspicion on stainless rigging screws, where salt water might wick down threads, plastic-covered stainless lifelines, swaged terminals, and many other important fittings, and inspect them regularly for signs of corrosion.

Staysail Stay, Movable The best wire for a movable staysail stay or baby stay is 7 x 7 stainless steel (seven strands of seven wires each). It's more flexible and less likely to work-harden than the usual 1 x 19 rigging wire (one strand of 19 wires).

Stern Glands, Rate of Drip If your boat has the kind of stern gland that drips water to lubricate the packing, the rule of thumb is to err on the side of too many drips per minute rather than too few.

The water flow is needed not only to lubricate the gland, but also to prevent an excessive buildup of heat. With the propeller shaft not turning, you should aim for a rate of about four drops a minute with new packing. When this has bedded in after about 10 or 15 hours of running, adjust the stuffing box gland for a rate of about one or two drops a minute. When the shaft is turning, the rate tends to be somewhat greater.

Sun, Distance Away The sun is 93 million miles from the earth, on average. It therefore takes light from the sun 8.3 minutes to reach the earth, traveling at 186,000 miles per second.

This means we see the sun in our sextants not as it is now, but how it was more than eight minutes ago. In fact, we have no idea, at this very instant, whether the sun still exists or not. However, the navigator should not let such niggling details affect his or her calculations. Due allowance for all this has been made by the clever astronomers who compile nautical tables and almanacs.

Swigging Swigging is the old term for putting far greater tension in a line, particularly a halyard, than would be possible with a straight pull.

To swig a halyard, hoist it as tightly as you can in the normal manner and then take a half turn around the cleat to prevent its slipping. With the other hand, grasp the halyard as high as you reasonably can and pull it out away from the mast. Then take up the slack you have won in this way by pulling the lower end of the halyard quickly around the cleat. It requires some dexterity and timing but it is a valuable skill that comes quickly with practice. Two people working together, one swigging and the other taking up the slack, can very quickly set up a halyard bar-taut.

S

165

T

Tacking, Downwind, Advantages of In displacement hulls, it usually pays to tack downwind in medium or light weather. In heavy weather there's little or no speed advantage.

Sailing 20 degrees off to one side of the true wind, and then 20 degrees back to the rhumb line, adds about 6 percent to the distance covered. If, by filling your jib, you can increase your speed by 6 percent (say from 4 knots to 4.24 knots), you'll arrive at the same time as the straight-line ETA.

If your speed increases by one-quarter of a knot to 4.25 knots, you'll get there sooner. In heavy weather, however, a hull is probably already forging ahead at maximum rate dead downwind and there would be no speed advantage to tacking downwind.

In light-displacement planing or semi-planing hulls, it pays to tack downwind in almost all weather conditions, all other things being equal.

Tacking, to Windward, Increased Distance On average, tacking to a windward destination increases the distance traveled by 40 percent of the straight-line distance.

Teak, Whether to Varnish The choices are to paint it, to varnish it, to dress it with oil, or to leave it to weather au naturel.

Few modern members of Western civilization can bring themselves to paint expensive teak instead of varnishing it, even when confronted season after season by the obvious sense of painting and the blatant stupidity of varnishing. It has a lot to do with yachting fashion and a little to do with the human soul.

Decks are best left to weather to a silvery gray, though some boat owners obsessed with the very thought of owning teak insist on regular but unnecessary sanding and staining with special sealers and oils.

Teak is naturally oily and soft. It's easily worn into grooves by too much scouring with the grain. In its natural form it provides a wonderful wet footgrip. Varnished or oiled, it becomes as treacherously slippery as any inferior wood.

A little varnished teak above decks sets a boat off, gives her the glow of a cherished object, and compensates to some extent for the plastic sterility of fiberglass. But too much is murder on her crew, or on her owner's pocketbook, and is a sign of poor judgment.

Down below, it's fashionable to leave teak unpainted to show the world that it *is* teak. Painted teak, after all, has no more obvious social standing than does painted pine.

Too often, though, vast surfaces of varnished or oiled teak make an otherwise pleasant interior resemble a gloomy 18th-century railway carriage. My preference is for lots of bright white surfaces down below, set off by varnished or oiled teak trim.

Builders like acres of teak because it's easy to work with and quick to finish with oil. Painted and varnished finishes need a lot more labor.

T

167

Tender, Ideal for Yacht The ideal yacht tender exists only in dreams. She should be small to stow on deck, but large to carry crew and provisions. She should be light to handle, but heavy to ride the seas. She should be wide for stability, but narrow for

ease of rowing. And so on. Here are L. Francis
Herreshoff's rules of thumb:

- She should row easily when light and when
  loaded.

- She should be light enough to be hoisted aboard
  easily.

- She should be stiff enough to get into and out of
  easily.

- She should be so constructed that she will not
  leak—and still will be able to stand some
  abuse.

- Last, but not least, she should tow steadily,
  always holding back on her painter and never
  yawing around.

Through-Hull Fittings, Precautions Hoses
attached to through-hull fittings are traditionally
fastened with two stainless-steel hose clips. But the
rule of thumb is that the innermost clip, the one far-
thest from the hull, should not be screwed up as
tightly as is the outboard one.

Boatyards often find hoses damaged by overtight-
ened clips that cover only half or less of the through-
hull fitting. On many through-hulls, there isn't
really room for two clips, side by side, on the barbed
pipe that the hose slips over. But it's wise to have a
spare already fitted, as long as it's not damaging the
hose.

Another rule for through-hulls is to keep a
tapered soft-wood plug next to each one to plug the
hole in an emergency. But don't use pine. It doesn't
swell (and jam in place) quickly enough.

Thumb, Original Rule of *See*: DANGERS, KEEP-
ING CLEAR OF

Thunder, Distance off The distance between
you and a thunderstorm in miles can be calculated
by dividing by 5 the number of seconds between the

lightning flash and the noise of the accompanying thunder.

Thunderstorms, Most Likely Times of
Over inland and coastal waters, thunderstorms are most common in the late afternoon and early evening. At sea, well away from land, they mostly occur between midnight and daybreak.

Tidal Streams, Average Strength
The average strength of a six-hour tidal stream is two-thirds of the maximum; the total drift in nautical miles is two-thirds of the maximum rate in knots multiplied by 6.

Tidal Streams, General Rules
In most locations the flow of the ebb tide is stronger and lasts longer than the flood. Another good rule of thumb is that you can expect strong tidal streams where two bays meet. And, when you're near the coast you'll generally find that the flood and ebb don't flow toward and away from the shore, but run parallel with it. A tidal stream is usually stronger within two or three miles of the shore than it is farther out.

Tidal Streams, Slack and Stand
Slack water occurs when there is no longer any discernible horizontal flow of current at the change of tide. Stand is the cessation of movement by the tide in a vertical direction—in other words, when it's no longer rising or falling.

T

169

Strangely enough, the two do not usually coincide. Tidal streams do not automatically stop flowing when the tide reaches its highest or lowest point. In fact, the water level can be falling for an hour or more while the stream is still flooding. If there is one truly valid rule of thumb about tides and tidal streams, it is that they are always vastly more complicated and unfathomable than you would expect.

Tides, Daily Variation in Time
The most common type of tide, the semidiurnal tide with two

high waters and two low waters every 24 hours, occurs about 50 minutes later each day.

Tides, Equinoctial Watch out for tides that are higher than normal high and lower than normal low at or near the equinoxes—that is, around March 21 and September 21.

Equinoctial tides display an unusually large tidal range, especially when a full or new moon is in or near the equinoctial, and particularly if the moon is at its perigee. Then the sun and the moon combine most effectively to attract the seas into the upward swelling bulge that causes tides.

Tides, Spring and Neap Ranges Spring tides have a range (the difference in height between high water and low water) about 20 percent greater than average. Neap tides have a range about 20 percent less than average.

Tides, the Twelfths Rule A semidiurnal tide rises (or falls) a predictable amount of its total range in every passing hour. After high (or low) water, the tide falls (or rises) the following amounts:

First hour:	$\frac{1}{12}$
Second hour:	$\frac{2}{12}$
Third hour:	$\frac{3}{12}$
Fourth hour:	$\frac{3}{12}$
Fifth hour:	$\frac{2}{12}$
Sixth hour:	$\frac{1}{12}$

The easy way to remember the twelfths rule is: 1-2-3-3-2-1. That adds up to 12. You can see that the tide rises (or falls) half ($\frac{6}{12}$) of its entire range in just two hours in the middle of a six-hour tide, and slows right down toward high water and low water. Tidal currents sometimes vary accordingly, but frequently are affected by other factors.

Tiller, Ideal Handgrip The experience of boatbuilders is that most people prefer the handgrip for a tiller to be round in section and 1¼ inches in diameter.

Another long-established rule of thumb is that the tiller shouldn't break if a 200-pound sailor falls on it. Any crewmember heavier than that should be requested to stay well clear of the tiller when likely to fall down.

See also: APPENDIX: TILLERS, MINIMUM SECTIONS OF

Time, Estimating In counting time intervals between 5 and 30 seconds, people who have not practiced the art of time estimation are out by an average of 16 percent.

You can improve your judgment of time between 1 and 30 seconds (the period mostly likely to be of use to boaters) by using a watch as a control. Most people find it easier to count two fairly deliberate beats to the second: "Oh one, oh two...oh nine, one oh, one one...two oh, two one..." You should be able to achieve 90-percent accuracy with a little practice.

Time Signals for Navigation Time signals from U.S. radio stations WWV and WWVH can be received almost anywhere in the world on frequencies of 2.5, 5, 10, 15, 20, and 25 MHz.

The service is continuous. Station WWV is located near Fort Collins, Colorado, and WWVH is in Kekaha-Kawai, Hawaii. Both are operated by the National Bureau of Standards in cooperation with the Naval Observatory.

T

171

Long-distance voyagers needing to check their chronometers will also find the British Broadcasting Corporation's hourly time signals useful. The BBC's World Service uses six "pips" to count down the last five seconds to the hour before newscasts. Any ordinary shortwave radio will do.

Tonnage, Different Determinations of
The tonnage of ships and boats can be expressed as a weight or as an interior volume without regard to weight.

Gross tonnage is a volume. It's the total enclosed space or internal capacity of a vessel expressed in units of 100 cubic feet, which are referred to as *tons*.

Net (or registered) tonnage is gross tonnage, less the volume of interior spaces that will not hold cargo. In the case of pleasure boats, deductions from gross tonnage would mainly be for engine compartments and control stations.

Displacement tonnage is the actual weight of the boat in long tons of 2,240 pounds each. It can be calculated by finding the volume of the vessel below the waterline in cubic feet and dividing by 35 (35 cubic feet of seawater weighs 1 long ton).

Deadweight tonnage, like net tonnage, is an indication of a vessel's cargo-carrying capacity; but whereas gross and net tonnages are volumes, deadweight tonnage is measured in long tons.

Trade Goods, Suggestions for

Mariners planning voyages to foreign countries, especially the lesser developed countries, would do well to remember the very basic rule of thumb for successful trading, which is to transport goods from places where they are cheap and plentiful to places where they are scarce and desirable.

Thus, on some dry islands in the Sea of Cortez, jugs of drinking water can readily be traded for fresh seafood. Fish hooks will buy you fresh fruit and services on remote South Pacific atolls. Drill bits, hacksaw blades, sewing needles, diesel fuel—all are in short supply somewhere.

Try to find out in advance what is needed at the places on your itinerary, and use your imagination as well. Use caution, though, because trade is well regulated everywhere by bureaucrats, and what you're trying to do is probably illegal.

Finally, never forget that dollar bills, the most universal trading goods of all, work wonders in most places, legally or illegally.

Traffic Separation Schemes, Navigation

of The rule of thumb is that traffic separation schemes marked on charts at the approaches to busy ports are meant to make navigation safer and more predictable for large or less maneuverable ships. They weren't put there for the benefit of small pleasure craft.

Boats smaller than 66 feet in length, including sailboats, must give way to larger traffic in traffic separation lanes and the zones where such lanes meet or cross.

Stay clear of them if you can. Stay near an outside edge if you *must* use them, so that you can give way to overtaking ships by moving slightly outside the limits of the lane temporarily. Usually there's plenty of water for small craft outside of the lanes. Don't be tempted to use the central separation zone because it looks so peaceful there. It's designed to be free of traffic.

You may cross a traffic separation scheme, including the central separation zone, any time you wish, but you should do so at right angles to the flow of the traffic. Keep a very sharp lookout, give way to everything approaching in a traffic lane, and don't underestimate the time needed to cross this maritime freeway. Some separation schemes are five miles wide.

Also keep a sharp eye on maverick ships who choose not to use the separation scheme. Although one-way traffic schemes mostly are intended for use by vessels of 300 gross tons and over, it's not usually obligatory to do so. Ships that choose not to use the schemes are, however, asked to stay well clear of them.

Trysail, Area of

Few modern cruising sailboats carry a storm trysail because the superior strength of Dacron, compared with old cotton or canvas sailcloth, enables a more convenient reefed mainsail to

T

173

be used in heavy weather instead. However, traditionalists insisting upon carrying separate storm trysails should know that they should have an area slightly less than that of the close-reefed mainsail. And a row of reef-points on the trysail probably wouldn't hurt, either.

Twin-Screw Installations In general, two engines are not twice as good as one, whether they be inboards or outboards. As a rule, twin-screw installations are comparatively wasteful of power. They also cost far more, need larger fuel tanks, require more servicing, and weigh far more. Furthermore, twin-engine inboard installations are commonly very cramped and leave little room for access, thus almost guaranteeing that the engines will be poorly maintained.

The commonest reason for having twin engines is safety. But it doesn't always work out that way. Many twin-screw, planing-hull powerboats are almost unmanageable under one engine in really heavy weather, when engine failure is most likely to occur.

What is often overlooked is the fact that a boat with two 100-h.p. engines cannot make the same use of all the available power as a boat with one 200-h.p. engine. Added weight, added friction in drivetrains, and added underwater drag from extra struts and rudders are formidable prices to pay. The rule of thumb is that a twin-screw installation wastes about 20 percent of the power available, compared with a single-engined installation of comparable horsepower.

These are very good reasons why you'll hardly ever see a commercial fishing boat of the long-range, displacement type with twin engines.

U

Upkeep, Estimating Costs Francis S. Kinney asks in *Skene's Elements of Yacht Design*: "Just how much is the upkeep per year? Not many owners will tell you—they don't want their wives to know."

Nevertheless, he offers a couple of well-informed guesses. Assuming that the owner does little or no maintenance for himself or herself, these are reasonable annual costs for upkeep, based on the original cost of the boat:

Wooden and steel boats: 5 to 12 percent

Aluminum and fiberglass boats: 2 to 5 percent

If Kinney's figures seem optimistically low (and I know they do to some) the fault probably lies in failing to adjust the original cost for inflation. These percentages might be about right for the first couple of years of a boat's life, but they'd probably be more accurate over the long haul if the original cost of the boat were adjusted upward for annual inflation.

Useless Articles on a Boat, the Three or Four Most Among modern boaters it's generally accepted (perhaps unfairly in at least one case) that the three most useless things aboard a yacht are:

- A stepladder
- An umbrella
- A naval officer

But a much older rule declared: "Four things shalt thou not see aboard a yacht for its comfort—a cow, a wheelbarrow, an umbrella, and a naval officer."

V

Varnish, Number of Coats Brightwork requires between 8 and 10 coats of varnish for that professional look.

Much as we all like to deceive ourselves, there is no shortcut to first-class brightwork. The rules are simple: Sand the wood smooth, fill the grain if necessary, and seal. Then apply 10 coats, sanding lightly between each and allowing each to dry completely before applying the next.

Immediately before varnishing, wipe sanding dust away with a tack cloth damped with a compatible thinner. Don't work outside when it's too hot, too cold, or too damp. Don't stir the varnish in the can or you'll introduce bubbles. Swirl it gently in the can to mix it, if you feel you have to, but mostly it isn't necessary.

Pour varnish from the can through a fine filter (cheesecloth or discarded nylon stocking) into a small container, and work from that. I prefer brushes, some of which I've had for 10 years or more, but many professionals use throw-away foam applicators, which does away with tedious brush-cleaning. Flow the varnish on; don't scrape it thin.

Incidentally, varnish often fails prematurely because the sun striking through it causes deterioration of the wood beneath. The usual suspect— ultraviolet radiation—is the culprit here, so for outside work choose a varnish that incorporates an ultraviolet radiation inhibitor.

Experts will tell you that it's not the kind of varnish you use that counts, it's the number of coats you apply. Of course, if you're the slightest bit brighter than your brightwork, you'll *paint* the outside wood and escape completely the dreadful tyranny of the varnishing regime.

Varnish, When to Scrape Down
Nobody with any sense scrapes down and revarnishes unless absolutely necessary.

For a while, you can get away with *patching*, or rubbing down a small area and varnishing over it to disguise the injury. Specifically, you can do this for shallow scratches and abrasions—perhaps even for deeper scratches—but you *must* do it before water, fresh or salt, soaks into the wood.

In the passage of time, you'll notice darker patches where water has discolored the wood and lighter patches where the varnish has lifted away from the wood because of the action of the sun or the impact of some piece of equipment on deck.

Some defiant owners try to treat dark patches with a mild bleach such as oxalic acid. They sand the white patches down to bare wood and build up several coats.

But they know in their hearts that they're fighting a rearguard action. Personal conscience is the best guide to when it's time to scrape the whole darned lot down to bare wood and start from scratch. When your brightwork is suffering from the pox and you can't live with it a minute longer, your conscience will nag you into action.

V

177

Varnish, When to Touch Up
Here's an old rule of thumb for telling when you need to sand down and apply a couple of coats of varnish to "freshen" your brightwork for the season:

Wash the work thoroughly to get rid of all grime. Wet a piece of old toweling cloth and drag it, dripping, across the surface of the varnish.

If the water left behind forms beads, the varnish work is still in good condition. If the water *sheets*, or lies in flattish streaks, the brightwork needs attention.

Ventilation, Increasing Efficiency
A 4-inch-diameter ventilation cowl passes almost twice as much air as does one with a diameter of 3 inches.

Those with long memories might recall that the area of a circle = πr^2, or 3.1416 times radius squared.

Ventilation, Natural, of Sailboats
The natural flow of air in most sailboats is from aft forward. It seems to matter very little which way the wind is blowing. Even when it's from ahead, the tendency is for fresh air to enter through the main hatch and exit through the fore hatch.

When arranging fans or additional ventilators, the aim should be to reinforce this natural air circulation, not to fight it.

Incidentally, I have never understood why yacht designers don't use hollow masts as ventilation ducts. They stand up there, high in the sky where there's plenty of wind, so why not fit baffled inlets on the foreside, and outlets in the bilges or the cabin?

Surely it's not beyond the ingenuity of mast engineers to design a really cheap and effective ventilation system, either forcing fresh air into the boat, or sucking old air out?

Ventilation is of such vital importance that I can't imagine why the potential of the mast to deliver a steady stream of fresh air has been ignored for so long.

Voices, Illusion of Hearing
Many people hear voices or music at sea while alone on watch at night. This is not truly an illusion, or necessarily the result of mental fatigue. It's a natural and normal occurrence that results from the ear's ability to filter noises.

The noise of the wind and the sea in stormy

weather contains a broad spectrum of almost all possible frequencies in random combinations. The ear and the brain between them highlight the frequencies that are of significance to survival—such as those in the range of human speech—and suppress the rest.

See also: HALLUCINATIONS, OCCURRENCE OF

Voyage, Definition of When Cape Horn sailors talked of a voyage, they meant the full journey, outward and return. A trip between any two ports en route was not a voyage but a passage.

W

Watches, the Seven Parts of the Day In the old tradition, a ship's crew was divided into two watches who split the day at sea into seven watch periods and worked watch-on, watch-off. The watch periods were:

Middle Watch:	Midnight to 4 AM
Morning Watch:	4 AM to 8 AM
Forenoon Watch:	8 AM to noon
Afternoon Watch:	Noon to 4 PM
First Dog Watch:	4 PM to 6 PM
Second Dog Watch:	6 PM to 8 PM
First Watch:	8 PM to midnight

Bells were struck for every half-hour of each watch, with a maximum of eight bells. At the end of the First Dog Watch, only four bells were struck, of course, and then the bells of the Second Dog Watch were struck like this: 6:30 PM, one bell; 7 PM, two bells; 7:30 PM, three bells; 8 PM, eight bells.

Since 1915, all U.S. merchant vessels over 100 tons gross have by law divided the crew into three watches, working four hours on and eight hours off, and turning the dog watches into one evening watch.

Pleasure boaters have rung many changes on this traditional system, which make it more convenient for small boats sailing shorthanded.

Water, Danger of Receding If you're *ashore* when the sea suddenly and mysteriously recedes, exposing abnormally large areas of beach, flee for the hills. If you're *aboard* and still floating at anchor, make all haste to the open sea, or at least to deep water.

The first noticeable part of the seismic sea wave known as a *tsunami* is the trough that causes the sea to recede from a beach. The approaching tidal wave can assume disastrous proportions on a shelving coast, but its effects in deep water are minimal because its height is usually only a few feet.

The speed of a wave can reach 300 to 500 knots, and its length 100 miles. Tsunamis, the result of underwater earthquakes, usually consist of a series of waves with crests 10 to 40 minutes apart. The highest might arrive several hours after the first wave.

Water, Drinking A supply of half a U.S. gallon per person per day is adequate—for drinking and cooking only—if supplemented by soft drinks and canned juices. A gallon a day is preferable if it's the sole source of potable liquid.

You can, and surely will, get by on less, depending on the outside weather and temperature. But providing between half a gallon and a gallon a day for each person, for the projected duration of an ocean passage covering an average of 100 miles a day, automatically assures you of an emergency reserve. An important rule is to divide the water supply among separate tanks or containers in case some of it should go bad or leak away.

W

181

When abroad, don't forget that the U.S. gallon is only four-fifths of the old British or Imperial gallon— 16 fluid ounces, compared to 20 fluid ounces. Most of the British Commonwealth has gone over to liters now, but world voyagers might still find isolated pockets of resistance to metrication where Imperial gallons rule the roost.

Good water will remain sweet for at least six months in tightly sealed containers, provided the containers are not quite full and are stowed out of the sun.

Water, Drinking, Purifying with Bleach

Voyagers topping up their tanks with fresh water from questionable sources need to sterilize it before use. A quick and convenient way is to add ordinary household liquid chlorine bleach. The rule of thumb is to add one teaspoonful of 5.25 percent bleach to every 15 gallons of water. This is more than the amount you'll find in public drinking water, which contains about one part of chlorine per million parts of water, but it's much easier to calculate.

Common bleaches, such as the widely known Clorox, contain a weak solution (about 5.25 percent) of sodium hypochlorite, which does its work and then breaks down within about 10 minutes of being exposed to light and air.

Leave the filler cap off your tank for 30 minutes to an hour or so, if you're able to, and the chlorine taste will disappear. Be cautious when first tasting: Chlorine will burn your mouth and throat if you use too much. Or, draw the water from the tank and let it sit, exposed to the air, for 30 minutes before you use it.

Be aware that this is not a permanent treatment. Because the chlorine is able to break down and dissipate on contact with air (unlike the chlorine in the pipes of a domestic water supply) your newly sterilized water is vulnerable to algae infestation and bacterial contamination almost immediately again. The answer is to repeat the sterilization at regular intervals, according to your particular circumstances, and always when taking aboard water from a supply of dubious purity.

When cleaning and flushing a water tank, a cupful of 5.25 percent liquid bleach for every 50 gallons will do a good job if left to stand for 10 minutes. Pump it through all your faucets and pipes before it loses its potency.

Two warnings:

- Chlorine corrodes stainless steel. If you have stainless tanks or fittings, allow the chlorine to break down quickly by exposing the water surface to fresh air.

- Never add bleach to tanks connected to a reverse osmosis water maker. The chlorine will do it no good at all.

Waterplane Area Several useful calculations start with waterplane area. It's simply the area of a horizontal slice through the hull at water level. For a close approximation, multiply waterline length by waterline beam, and then multiply the result by 0.76.

To find how much your boat will sink in the water when you add weight, simply multiply her waterplane area in square feet by 5.34. The result is the number of pounds needed to sink her 1 inch.

Waterspouts, Recognition of Skeins of rain falling from a distant cloud often direct a mariner's thoughts to waterspouts, which, although less violent than their landlubber cousins, tornadoes, still represent a real danger to small craft. Like a tornado, a waterspout forms beneath a rain cloud, a cumulonimbus. It starts as a funnel-shaped extension of the cloud base, growing down to a sea surface whipped into clouds of spray. Then it merges with the spray and joins the cloud base to the sea surface with a narrow tunnel.

Waterspouts vary from 20 to 200 feet across, and can stretch from sea-level to a cloud 1,000 or 2,000 feet up. They usually last between 10 and 30 minutes, becoming more and more bent and elongated until the tube breaks open, upon which the system quickly collapses.

If it looks like you'll get caught in one in a sailboat, take down all sail, fold down your dodger,

W

183

secure everything loose on deck, go below, and slide your hatches tightly shut. A powerboat should have less difficulty staying clear of a waterspout.

Wave Height, Estimating

The trouble with trying to estimate the size of ocean waves is that *down* isn't always down at sea. The scientist William Froude started investigating this phenomenon in 1861. Basically, what happens is that waves produce accelerations that combine with gravity to produce a local *down* that is oriented squarely onto the surface of the water. In other words, no matter where you are on the slope of a wave, *down* always seems to be at right angles to the surface.

No amount of mental compensation can get things into perspective because the illusion of *down* arises from real physical forces to which humans have been conditioned to respond over the centuries. Still, knowing it exists can help explain why an apparently near-vertical avalanche of water rearing up astern seems to flatten out and pass harmlessly beneath the hull.

The rule of thumb that has arisen from these scientific observations is that the real sea is probably not much more than half as high, or as steep, as it looks at its worst moment.

The only reasonable way to estimate the height of the waves is to wait until you are truly in the trough, midway between crests, when most crests will be even with the horizon in all directions. Your perception of the sea height at that brief moment will be untainted by illusion.

Wave Length, Velocity and Period

The relationship between the size and speed of waves is approximately this:

- Length equals velocity times period.
- Period equals velocity divided by 5⅛.

Another method of finding the period is to take

the length and divide it by 5⅛. Then take the square root of the answer.

Waves, Height of, in Gales
As previously noted, the height of waves is extremely difficult to estimate from the deck of a small boat in heavy weather. At the same time, there is often a natural tendency to exaggerate. So sailors' accounts of wave heights are traditionally taken with a pinch of salt. Nevertheless, carefully gathered scientific data indicate that wave heights of between 40 and 50 feet are not uncommon in heavy gales in some oceans.

There are, however, many reports of single waves much bigger. A wave 80 feet high was observed from the steamship *Majestic* in the North Atlantic at 48 30N, 21 50W, on December 29, 1922. Meteorological authorities considered the sighting authentic.

Of more interest to small boats, however, is the height of the breaking crests. It's safe to assume that in a whole gale (48 to 55 knots) in the open sea, many breakers of 6 feet in height will spill down the fronts of waves.

See also: BREAKERS, SPILLING AND PLUNGING

Waves, Height of in the Open Sea
The relationship between wind speed, in miles per hour, and wave height, in feet, is approximately 2 to 1.

This ratio from the U.S. Hydrographic Office indicates that a wind of 50 mph should raise a 25-foot sea.

W

The length of a wave, from crest to crest, is about 20 times the height. So, a wave 25 feet high would have a length of about 500 feet and a speed (square root of length times 1.34) of about 30 knots.

Waves, Maximum, Size of Fetch Needed for
For waves to grow to their maximum size, a *fetch* (a stretch of deep water unaffected by land masses) of about 600 miles is required. Thus, for the same wind speed, the waves off Cape Horn should be

no greater than those off the northwest coast of the United States.

The wind must also blow in the same direction for a certain minimum time for the sea to become fully developed, of course, and the rule of thumb here is that the time in hours equals the wind speed in knots. In other words, a 20-knot wind will take about 20 hours to form the biggest waves it can; and so on.

Waves, Motion of Water in We often hear that the water in a wave has no horizontal motion, but this is not entirely true. In fact, the water is actually moving forward at the top of a wave. In the hollow it moves backward and in the middle part of the slope it moves vertically up or down.

Waves, Speed of a Group of The speed of advance of a group of waves is half that of individual waves. When the wind dies down, the height of waves diminishes rapidly, but length and speed remain unchanged. The result is a swell that can travel for hundreds of miles and far outrun the disturbance that caused it.

Weather, Forecasting *See*: BAROMETER, CONVENTIONAL WISDOM CONCERNING; AND APPENDIX: WEATHER PROVERBS

Weather Helm, Benefits of Tank testing has shown that a small amount of weather helm, about 2 or 3 degrees, helps to lift a sailboat to windward. But if you have to apply 4 degrees or more, the rudder starts acting as a brake.

Weather helm, which is the need to hold the helm to weather to maintain a steady course, is used to counter the tendency of an unbalanced hull or rig to round up into the wind. Excessive weather helm is dangerous and makes a boat unseaworthy.

See also: GRIPING, CAUSES OF; AND BALANCED HELM, FACTORS AFFECTING MONOHULL SAILBOATS

Weatherliness, Improvements in These are average tacking angles to the true (not apparent) wind:

Viking longboat: 70 degrees

Square rigger: 70 degrees

Clipper ship: 65 degrees

Cruising yacht: 50 to 55 degrees

Racing yacht: 40 to 45 degrees

Weight, Crew and Stores, Estimates of

For planning purposes, the weight of crew and stores can be estimated as follows:

Crew: Multiply number of crew by 160 pounds.

Stores: Allow 6 pounds per person per day for food and packaging.

Water: Allow 8.5 pounds per person per day.

Safety reserve: Multiply the total of stores and water by 1.5 to allow for a reserve.

Personal gear: Allow 5 pounds per person per day of a cruise, up to a maximum of about 120 pounds. For permanent cruisers and liveaboards, a maximum of 500 to 1,000 pounds is nearer the mark.

See also: SIZE, DOWN BELOW

Weight-Carrying Capacity

A cruising sailboat fitted out for indefinite voyaging—longer than six months—should be capable of carrying 2,000 pounds per crewmember.

This includes everything short-term cruisers need, plus extra tools, books, clothing, food, water, and as many home comforts as stowage space permits.

W

Wheel Steering, Turns from Lock to Lock

The ideal number of turns for wheel steering, from lock to lock (that is, from 35 degrees port rudder to 35 degrees starboard rudder), is roughly:

Runabouts, small motorboats, and all sizes of fast powerboats: 1¾ to 2

Trawler-type motor cruisers, 30 to 50 feet in length: 2½ to 3½

**Trawler-type motor cruisers more than 50
feet in length:** 3½ to 4

**Sailboats up to 30 feet (if not feasible to fit
a tiller):** 1 to 2

Sailboats, 30 to 45 feet: 2 to 3

Sailboats, 50 feet and up: 3 to 5

Whistling and Bad Weather

The old rule was that a sailor never whistled on watch for fear of bringing bad weather.

He could whistle during his off watch, or even play the fiddle if he wanted to, but the theory was that any sailor who whistled when he was supposed to be working didn't have enough to do.

The gods of the wind and the sea were said to hate idlers (a rumor no doubt started deliberately by ship owners and captains), so they would soon provide him with an abundance of labor in the form of worsening weather.

There is a saying that only fools and bosun's mates whistle on deck. Bosun's mates could whistle with impunity because they were believed to be agents of the devil, particularly when they were wielding a cat-o'-nine-tails.

Winch, Size of

The most repeated rule of thumb about winches is that you should get the experts' recommendation for the correct size of winch for your application, and then buy one a size larger.

Work out the maximum load you want your winch to handle (*See:* SHEETS, HEADSAIL AND MAINSAIL, DIAMETER OF) and consult the manufacturer's catalog.

Most boats today carry two-speed or three-speed winches. The winch handle is wound one way for the first speed, and the opposite way for the second speed.

This enables the slack in a sheet, for example, to be taken in quickly at the first speed, and then trimmed more slowly under pressure at the second (or third) speed.

Wind Direction, Apparent, Changes with Altitude
When a boat is sailing, the apparent wind direction changes by between 5 and 8 degrees from the bottom of the mast to the top. Therefore, the rule of thumb is that the leech at the head of the sail should lie further off the wind than the leech near the clew.

This comes about because the wind velocity rises with altitude, where it is less and less affected by the friction of the sea. Thus, if the true wind speed is higher up aloft, the apparent wind direction up there is less affected by the boat's forward speed. It is nearer the true wind direction; so the top of the sail does not need to be sheeted so close to the wind as does the bottom. You don't have to worry about this, though. Your sailmaker knows about it and has built something like the correct twist and camber into your sail already.

Wind Direction, Changes, What They Portend
As a general rule, a backing wind (changing in a counterclockwise direction) in the Northern Hemisphere indicates the approach of bad weather. A veering wind (changing direction clockwise) signals the approach of better weather, but not necessarily immediately. In the Southern Hemisphere, bad weather usually follows a veering wind and good weather a backing wind.

You can find the center of a depression by facing directly into the wind. In the Northern Hemisphere, the low-pressure area is on your right and slightly behind you. In the Southern Hemisphere, it's on your left.

Wind Speed, Average While Voyaging
Approximately 65 percent of all ocean voyaging is done in winds of 12 knots or less.

That is an observation by Lin and Larry Pardey. The British world voyager Eric Hiscock said that during his three circumnavigations, the trade winds averaged Force 4 on the Beaufort Scale—between 11 and 16 knots.

W

Wind Speeds, Beaufort Scale of   As a general rule, sailors describe wind speeds by a number from 0 to 12 that indicates a range rather than a specific speed. The cipher 0 indicates a calm, and 12 a hurricane.

The scale was devised around 1805 by Sir Francis Beaufort, a British naval officer, and is also used by the World Meteorological Organization.

See also: APPENDIX: BEAUFORT SCALE OF WIND FORCES

Windlass, Definition of   A windlass is a winch, usually employed for weighing anchor, that has a horizontal barrel or barrels. Many yacht windlasses have two barrels: a smooth one with flanges for hauling on rope, known as a *gypsy*, and another with recesses for links of chain, known as a *wildcat*. A capstan, on the other hand, has a vertical barrel that, in bygone days, was turned by spikes fitted horizontally into holes around its head.

Winterizing, the Main Points   The word *winterization* is purposefully vague so as not to dishearten boaters by reminding them of the considerable amount of work to be done in laying up a boat for the winter in cold climates.

The basic rules about winterization all center on preventing corrosion or damage by wet or freezing weather. The main rule is: Look for where water lurks. Water that becomes ice and then thaws often breaks or bends out of shape whatever contained it.

Another important rule is to protect the vessel from rain, snow, and frost while allowing a copious stream of fresh air to flow through every nook and cranny. Good ventilation is more important than a roof or cover over the boat, if you have to choose.

Water lurks in some unexpected places on a boat. Look for it in U-bends under sinks. Look for it in sea cocks, holding tanks, and other places you don't often think about, for if you ignore it now it will surely take revenge one dark night when your back is turned.

Get rid of as much of it as you can. What remains must be dosed with antifreeze. A 50/50 solution of vodka is often used for drinking-water lines. Label the faucet, though, to avoid a surprise in spring.

What else? Clean the underwater hull immediately after she comes out of the water. Get all the marine growth off before it dries. Get the mast out and lay it on level sawhorses. Inspect, inspect, inspect.

That leaves the engine. Engine manufacturers all have their own specific instructions about winterizing, but the basic rules pertain:

Drain all raw-water systems. Check the antifreeze in a closed cooling system and renew it. Change the engine oil now, not at the beginning of the season. You don't want old oil, full of acids, eating away at your engine's insides all winter. Grease everything that can be greased. Turn the engine over without starting, and squirt some oil into the air intake manifold so that it coats the piston heads and cylinder walls.

Check sacrificial zincs and replace them now. You'll forget in spring. Plug all openings into the engine from the air intakes, the exhaust system, the breathers, and anywhere else, to keep out debris the engine doesn't like, including insects and small vermin. Paste up a big warning not to start the engine until all the plugs have been removed.

Disconnect the batteries and take them ashore for steady trickle charging. Sit quietly for 10 minutes and just *think* of what cold weather might do to your engine.

Then sit quietly for another 30 minutes and make a list of the general maintenance you plan to do through the winter, from taking the sails home and

W

191

washing them to greasing the sea cocks and strip-
ping the winches. Do it while you still clearly
remember what went wrong this summer. Won't
take you 30 minutes, you say? Uh-huh, that's what
they all say.

Wire Terminal Connectors Crimping electri-
cal wires to terminal connections is preferable to soldering them.

This might sound like heresy to old-timers, but it's
now the opinion of most competent authorities. The
major caveat is that the crimping must be done with
correctly sized crimping tools specified by the manufacturer of the terminal. After carefully cleaning
and crimping the joint, waterproof it and protect it
from salt air with an air-drying liquid vinyl or
shrink-wrap tubing.

Soldering often produces hard spots that can
cause flexing, fatigue, and breakage in the wire.
Solder is not as corrosion-proof as is commonly supposed, either. Salt air attacks it, leaving messy white
residue, little physical strength, and practically no
electrical integrity.

Wood, as a Boatbuilding Material Wood is
still as good a material for building boats as it ever
was.

It's stronger, pound for pound, than fiberglass. It's
stiffer, pound for pound, than steel, aluminum, or
fiberglass. It floats, it accepts fastenings well, it's
plentiful, it's easily repaired with simple tools, and
it's biodegradable. Furthermore, it's warm and
appealing to the human soul. Unfortunately, a
wooden boat cannot be mass produced as simply and
as cheaply from a standard mold as can a fiberglass
craft. In addition, wood makes a delectable meal for
a variety of hungry microbes, borers, and seaworms.

For a one-off hull, however, there's still nothing
to beat wood. There's an increasing tendency to seal
it during construction with several coats of epoxy

resin. Advocates assert that its rot resistance and longevity should compare well with fiberglass.

Epoxy coatings are efficient at blocking the passage of moisture into wood. The optimum water content of boatbuilding wood, by weight, is 15 percent. But the fungi that cause decay by feeding on the cellulose between the cell walls prefer a moisture content of 25 to 30 percent.

Without sufficient water, and lacking oxygen, fungi cannot grow inside epoxy-coated wood. At least, that's the theory.

In practice, although the water content of the wood might be expected to remain almost constant for many years, we all know that no epoxy coating blocks moisture totally.

That's why it's *not* advisable to coat thick timbers with epoxy. They have only to swell a little and the epoxy coating will split, allowing more water to enter and effectively become trapped there.

It's better to laminate thin pieces of timber so that each individual piece is isolated and encapsulated.

I personally have doubts about totally sealing wood with plastic resins. If at all possible, I paint one surface of the timber with ordinary oil-based paint that can "breathe" and thus allow trapped moisture to escape. I subscribe to the theory that no matter what you do, water will find its way in sooner or later, and you'd do better to provide a path for it to get out again.

W

193

Wooden Spars, Filling Cracks in Longitudinal cracks do not appreciably weaken a spar. They are, in fact, a sign that the wood is not "dead." The rule of thumb is that the cracks should not be filled with any material that sets hard. Here are two old recipes for homemade filler, the first for using cold, like putty, and the second for pouring in hot when the spar is horizontal. Whichever you choose, make sure the wood is thoroughly dry first.

- Warm a half-pint of linseed oil. Dissolve in it ½ pound of resin and ¼ pound of beeswax. Finally, add 3 ounces of turpentine.

- Melt together 1 pound of resin, ¼ pound of beeswax, and ¾ pint of linseed oil. Pour while still warm.

One presumes that common sense obviates the tedious necessity for warnings against eating the stuff or inviting a swift and carcinogenic demise by sniffing it while hot, etc.

Writers, Yachting, Rules for Here are the guiding principles for those who wish to write about pleasure boating, according to W. P. Stephens, boat-builder and author of *Traditions and Memories of American Yachting*:

> *A yachting writer should possess some sense of honesty and common decency, and he should first of all be a practical yacht sailor, familiar with handling and the rules. He should have a thorough knowledge of yachting history, as the present means nothing unless compared with the past; he should have some knowledge of the principles of yacht design and also of construction.*

Y

Yacht, Definition of   The definition in *Chapman's Piloting, Seamanship, and Small Boat Handling* is as good as any and has the distinct advantage of brevity:

> *A yacht is a power or sail vessel used for recreation and pleasure, as opposed to work.*

Z

Zinc, Sacrificial Zinc installed for marine corrosion protection should always meet military specifications or better. The standard is Mil-A-18001 J, but if the final letter is higher, that's better. Make sure you're not buying a lesser grade, or your zinc anodes might fail to give much-needed protection. And never paint over them.

Sacrificial zincs should be replaced every year. If they're working correctly, they should be about 50 percent eaten away by this time. If they're not, seek expert advice.

APPENDIX:
USEFUL TABLES AND FORMULAS

Anchors, Recommended Sizes These recommendations, taken from Earl Hinz's *The Complete Book of Anchoring and Mooring*, are general suggestions only—the size of a boat's anchors and gear depend on factors other than her overall length. In particular, the heavier the displacement of a boat and the more surface area she presents to the wind, the sturdier her ground tackle should be.

These are absolute minimum figures for average-profile boats of moderate displacement and beam. They're valid for working anchors in winds of up to 30 knots. Boats of more than average beam, or of heavy displacement, should carry anchors one size larger than those recommended here for their length.

The Herreshoff anchor referred to is the traditional type, which, although awkward to handle on deck, is superior to others on rocky or weed-covered bottoms. Cruising boats often carry an extra-large Herreshoff as an emergency storm anchor.

Anchor Type and Weight in Pounds

Boat Length (Feet)	Danforth Hi-Tensile	C.Q.R.	Bruce	Herreshoff
20	5	15	11	25
30	12	20	17	35
35	12	25	22	45
40	20	35	33	55
50	35	45	44	75
60	60	60	66	100

Adapted from *The Complete Book of Anchoring and Mooring*, 2nd ed., by Earl R. Hinz. Copyright© 1986, 1993 by Cornell Maritime Press, Inc. Used by permission

See also: APPENDIX: CHAIN, RECOMMENDED SIZES FOR ANCHOR CHAIN

Battery Capacity, Calculation of Needs

The amount of energy stored in batteries is usually rated in ampere-hours (commonly called amp-hours). You can calculate your average daily amp-hour requirements by listing all the items aboard your boat that consume DC electricity from your battery bank.

Note the number of watts used by each item and then estimate the number of hours, or portions of an hour, the item is in use each day. Where items are rated in amps rather than watts, multiply amps by battery voltage to get watts. Then multiply watts by hours, and you have your daily watt-hour requirements. Divide watt-hours by the battery voltage (usually 12) to get amp-hours.

For example:

Appliance	Watts	Hours	Watt-Hours
Anchor light	10	10	100.0
Bilge pump	48	0.2	9.6
Cabin fan	12	6	72.0
Cabin lights	48	5	240.0
Instruments	12	3	36.0
Inverter	60	4.3	258.0
FM/AM radio	2	4	8.0
Starter motor	2400	0.006*	14.4
SSB radio (on standby)	12	3	36.0
SSB radio (transmit)	240	0.3	72.0
Tape deck	15	4	60.0
VHF (receive)	6	12	72.0
VHF (transmit)	60	0.2	12.0
Water pump	48	0.25	12.0
Windlass	240	0.16	38.4

* Four starts lasting 5 seconds each
Total watt-hours: 1,040.4
On a 12-volt system, divide 1,040.4 by 12 to get amp-hours:
Total amp-hours: 86.7

Call this 90 amp-hours. Now, bear in mind the rule of thumb that only 40 percent of your total capacity is really usable. The resulting necessary battery capacity becomes 225 amp-hours (40 percent of 225 = 90).

If you were generous in your estimates, and determined to save more energy in future, you could probably settle for two batteries rated at 100 amp-hours each.

This means that each one, in theory, could supply 5 amps for 20 hours at 80 degrees F, or 20 amps for 5 hours, and so on. But we know better than that. It's difficult to top up the last 10 percent of a battery's capacity during ordinary recharging, and it isn't good for the life of the battery (even for a deep-cycle battery) to let it drop below 50 percent of capacity before recharging—hence the 40-percent rule of thumb.

It's always helpful, and frequently very illuminating, to work through this exercise and discover which appliances drain the most energy from the batteries. Notice that, despite its huge draw, the starter motor does not drain much energy from the battery because it's used for only seconds at a time. Appliances such as cabin lights—or, on a sportfishing boat, a bait-well pump—do the most damage with a fairly low draw over a long period. They often deceive you about the state of the battery, too. With the lights glowing reasonably brightly and the bait pump running well, your battery might be quite unable to start your engine because the voltage has dropped below a level acceptable to the starter motor. A 48-watt bait pump running for 10 hours will drain 40 amp-hours at 12 volts—that alone accounts for the total draw level on a 100-amp-hour battery under the 40-percent rule.

By the way, and this might sound obvious, but if you choose to increase your battery capacity, be sure you have the capacity to recharge the whole bank.

Your existing alternator might not be enough for the job.

If you have no way of ascertaining the wattage or amperage of an appliance on your boat, refer to the following table for a rough idea of average loads, in watts, on a 12-volt DC system:

Lights

Cabin lights, incandescent or fluorescent: 6 to 40 each

Navigation lights

Masthead (steaming) light: 12

Masthead tricolor: 24

Port, starboard, and stern: 12 each

Anchor light: 12 or 24

Other lights

Spreaders: 24 to 30 each

Strobe light: 9

Instruments

Automatic pilot: 40

Depthfinder (flasher type): 3

Depthfinder (recording strip): 6

GPS: 6 to 12

Instrument lights: 1 to 2

Loran: 6 to 12

Radio direction finders: 12

Radio, SSB (receive): 12

Radio, SSB (transmit): 240
Radio, VHF (receive): 6
Radio, VHF (transmit): 12 to 60
Radar: 50 to 240
Speed and windspeed instruments: 1 to 3 each
Weatherfax: 120

Equipment

Bilge or bait-well pump: 24 to 180
Blender: 30
Cabin fan: 12
Cabin heater (oil-fired): 100
Drill: 120
Engine starter motor: 5,400
Electric toilet: 200
Galley fan: 40
Microwave: 540
Pressure water pump: 84
Refrigerator: 84
Soldering iron (small): 60
Tape deck: 12 to 24
Vacuum cleaner: 120
Washing machine (mini): 60
Windlass: 240
Windshield wiper: 40

Beaufort Scale of Wind Forces

Beaufort Number	Wind Speed (Knots)	Description	Effects
0	under 1	Calm	Sea like a mirror
1	1 to 3	Light air	Slight ripples; sailboat just has steerage way
2	4 to 6	Light breeze	Small wavelets; wind just keeps sails filled
3	7 to 10	Gentle breeze	Large wavelets; sailboats begin to heel
4	11 to 16	Moderate breeze	Small waves; sailboats dip gunwales under water
5	17 to 21	Fresh breeze	Moderate waves, many whitecaps; time to reef
6	22 to 27	Strong breeze	Double-reefed mainsails; waves 8 to 12 feet

Beaufort Number	Wind Speed (Knots)	Description	Effects
7	28 to 33	Near gale	Waves 12 to 20 feet; foam starts blowing streaks
8	34 to 40	Gale	Waves 12 to 20 feet, but longer, with spindrift
9	41 to 47	Strong gale	High waves; spray starts to reduce visibility
10	48 to 55	Storm	Waves to 30 feet with overhanging crests
11	56 to 63	Violent storm	Waves to 45 feet; white foam patches cover sea
12	64 and over	Hurricane	Foam fills air; sea all white; waves over 45 feet

Breaking Strength of 1 x 19 Stainless Steel Rigging Wire

Diameter (Inches)	Pounds
⅛	2,100
⁵⁄₃₂	3,300
³⁄₁₆	4,700
⁷⁄₃₂	6,300
¼	8,200
⁹⁄₃₂	10,300
⁵⁄₁₆	12,500
⅜	17,600
⁷⁄₁₆	23,400
½	29,700
⁹⁄₁₆	37,000
⅝	46,800
¾	59,700
⅞	76,700

Breaking Strengths of Rope and Safe Working Load of BBB Chain (diameters in inches, strengths in pounds)

Diameter	Manila	Nylon	Dacron	Chain
³⁄₁₆	450	850	900	800
¼	600	1,100	1,200	1,325
⁵⁄₁₆	1,000	1,800	1,800	1,950
⅜	1,300	2,600	2,600	2,750
⁷⁄₁₆	1,700	3,700	3,500	3,625
½	2,600	5,000	4,500	4,750
⁹⁄₁₆	3,400	6,400	5,500	5,875
⅝	4,400	8,000	6,800	7,250
¾	5,400	10,500	9,300	10,250
⅞	7,700	14,000	12,600	12,000
1	9,000	18,800	16,100	15,000

Chain, Recommended Sizes for Anchor Chain

The following table lists the sizes, chosen by conservative designers, that have proved adequate for sailboats of average design and windage characteristics for more than 50 years. They are valid for BBB or short-link chain.

Enter the table with either boat length or displacement, whichever results in the greater weight of chain.

Boat Length (Feet)	Displacement (Pounds)	Chain Diameter (Inches)
25–30	5,000–10,000	¼
30–35	10,000–15,000	⁵⁄₁₆
35–40	15,000–20,000	⅜
40–45	20,000–30,000	⁷⁄₁₆
45–50	30,000–50,000	½
50–60	50,000+	⁹⁄₁₆

See also: APPENDIX: ANCHORS, RECOMMENDED SIZES

Collision Regulations for Power-Driven Vessels: Helpful Aids to Memory in Verse

> *Meeting steamers do not dread.*
> *When you see three lights ahead,*
> *Starboard wheel and show your red.*
>
> *Green to green or red to red,*
> *Perfect safety, go ahead.*
>
> *If to starboard red appear,*
> *'Tis your duty to keep clear;*
> *Act as judgment says is proper:*
> *Port—or starboard—back or stop her.*
>
> *But when upon your port is seen*
> *A steamer's starboard light of green,*
> *There's not so much for you to do,*
> *For green to port keeps clear of you.*
>
> *Both in safety and in doubt*
> *Always keep a good look-out;*
> *In danger with no room to turn,*
> *Ease her—Stop her—Go astern.*

Mercifully perhaps, I have no similar doggerel for sailing vessels. But here are the International and Inland Rules for Sailing Vessels, anyway.

Opposite-tack rule

When two sailing vessels approaching one another so as to involve risk of collision have the wind on different sides, the one having the wind on her port side shall keep out of the way of the one with the wind on the starboard side.

Same-tack rule

When both have the wind on the same side, the vessel to windward shall keep out of the way of the vessel to leeward.

In-doubt rule

If a sailing vessel with the wind on the port side sees a sailing vessel to windward and cannot determine with certainty whether the windward vessel has the wind on the port side or starboard side, she shall keep out of the way of the windward vessel.

Note: The rule defines the windward side as the side opposite that on which the mainsail is carried; or, if you're aboard a square-rigger, the side opposite that on which the largest fore-and-aft sail is carried.

Companionway Steps, Spacing and Slope

This is Francis S. Kinney's method of designing safe and comfortable steps, taken from *Skene's Elements of Yacht Design*:

1. Divide the vertical distance between deck and cabin sole into equal spaces of between 9 and 11 inches each.

2. Lay out the horizontal distance by allowing a projection forward of 9 inches for the top step and successive projections of 5 inches forward for each step thereafter.

3. Each step should be 6 inches from fore to aft, allowing an overlap of 1 inch.

Distance of Sea Horizon

Height of Eye or Light In Feet	Distance in Nautical Miles	Height of Eye or Light In Feet	Distance in Nautical Miles
1	1.1	31	6.4
2	1.6	32	6.5
3	2.0	33	6.6
4	2.3	34	6.7
5	2.6	35	6.8
6	2.8	36	6.9
7	3.0	37	7.0
8	3.2	38	7.1
9	3.4	39	7.1
10	3.6	40	7.2
11	3.8	41	7.3
12	4.0	42	7.4
13	4.1	43	7.5
14	4.3	44	7.6
15	4.4	45	7.7
16	4.6	46	7.8
17	4.7	47	7.8
18	4.9	48	7.9
19	5.0	49	8.0
20	5.1	50	8.1
21	5.2	55	8.5
22	5.4	60	8.9
23	5.5	65	9.2
24	5.6	70	9.6
25	5.7	75	9.9
26	5.8	80	10.2
27	5.9	85	10.5
28	6.1	90	10.9
29	6.2	95	11.2
30	6.3	100	11.4

Distress Signals In an emergency, you can and should use any means you like to summon help. Here are the signals recommended in the International and Inland Rules:

- Gun or other explosive signal fired at intervals of about a minute

- Continuous sounding of any fog signaling apparatus

- Red meteor flares

- Red parachute flares

- Red hand-held flares

- Flames, as from a substance burning in a metal bucket

- Orange smoke signal

- Dye marker in water (any color)

- Raising and lowering your arms slowly and repeatedly

- International code flags N over C

- International code letters N and C (— . — . — .) sent by Morse

- Any approximately square object over any approximately round object, such as a flag over a ball

- Black square and ball on an orange background

- The letters SOS, using any method, including radio, sound, or light

- The spoken word *Mayday* sent by radio

- Automatic signals sent by an EPIRB, radio-telephone, or radio-telegraph.

In addition, the Inland Rules (only) list a white high-intensity strobe light flashing 50 to 70 times a minute.

Don't forget that a cellular telephone can also bring you help if you dial 911 almost anywhere in the United States.

Flags, International Single-Letter Code

These flags, flown singly, have meanings that are understood all over the world. Each single-letter code is a complete signal when flown as a flag or transmitted by any method, including Morse:

A   I have a diver down; keep well clear at low speed.

B   I am carrying a dangerous cargo. (Or, if flown by a racing yacht, an indication that she has protested a breach of the rules.)

C   Affirmative. Yes.

D   Keep clear of me. I am maneuvering with difficulty.

E   I am altering my course to my starboard.

F   I am disabled. Communicate with me.

G   I require a pilot.

H   I have a pilot on board.

I   I am altering course to my port.

J   I am on fire and have dangerous cargo on board. Keep well clear.

K   I wish to communicate with you.

L   You should stop your vessel instantly.

M   I am stopped and making no way through the water.

N   Negative. No.

O   Person overboard.

P   In harbor: All persons should report on board as the vessel is about to proceed to sea. At sea, aboard fishing vessels: My nets have come fast upon an obstruction.

Q   My vessel is healthy and I request free pratique (that is, permission to do business at a port, or to make use of its amenities).

R   (Spare. No meaning has been assigned to this flag.)

S   I am operating astern propulsion.

T   Keep clear of me. I am engaged in pair-trawling.

U   You are running into danger.

V   I require assistance.

W   I require medical assistance.

X   Stop carrying out your intentions and watch for my signals.

Y   I am dragging my anchor.

Z   I require a tow. Or, when made by fishing vessels operating close to each other: I am shooting nets.

Galvanic Series From the anodic (or least noble, or most active, or sacrificial) end, to the cathodic (or most noble, or least active, or protected) end. The current flow is from magnesium toward platinum.

Magnesium

Galvanized iron and steel

Zinc

Cadmium

Aluminum (Marine alloys 5086, 5083, and 6061)

Mild steel

Aluminum (forged alloy)

Wrought iron

Cast iron

Stainless steel (oxygen-starved)

Lead

Tin

Manganese bronze

Phosphor bronze

Brass

Copper

Gunmetal

Silicon bronze

Tin bronze

Copper/nickel

Aluminum bronze

Stainless steel (in oxygen)

Monel metal

Titanium

Silver

Gold

Mercury

Graphite and carbon

Platinum

Halyard Sizes for Average Applications for 7 x 19 stainless steel wire rope:

Length of Mainsail Luff or Headsail Leech (Feet)	Size of Topping Lift or Main Halyard (Inches)
20–25	$\frac{1}{8}$
30–35	$\frac{5}{32}$
40–45	$\frac{3}{16}$
50–60	$\frac{7}{32}$
65–80	$\frac{1}{4}$

For headsail halyards, sizes should be $\frac{1}{32}$ inch larger.
For spinnaker halyards, sizes should be $\frac{1}{16}$ inch larger.

For double-braided Dacron rope:
All-rope halyards should be the same size as the sheet for the largest sail expected to be hoisted by that halyard.

See also: SHEETS, HEADSAIL AND MAINSAIL, DIAMETER OF

211

Horsepower Generated by Sails, Approximate

Wind Strength	Wind Speed (Knots)	h.p./Square Foot
Force 3	7–10	0.015
Force 4	11–16	0.020
Force 5	17–21	0.040
Force 6	22–27	0.070

Lead Line Markings, Traditional, for Large Ships

These are some of the standard markings used by square-rig sailors. The marks could be distinguished in the dark by the sense of feel on the fingers or lips. Note that not every fathom was marked. Depths that were not near a mark were estimated or measured by outstretched arms (traditionally one fathom); these unmarked fathom intervals were known as *deeps*. At two fathoms, for example, the leadsman would call "By the mark, twain." At eleven fathoms, he would call "Deep Eleven."

Marked Depths (Fathoms)	Marks
2	leather with two ends
3	leather with three ends
5	white calico
7	red bunting
10	flat leather with a hole
13	thick blue serge
15	white calico again
17	red bunting again
20	cord with two knots
25	cord with one knot
30	cord with three knots
35	cord with one knot again
40	cord with four knots, etc.

Lead Line Markings, Graham and Tew's Improved System for Boaters

1 fathom	1 piece of leather bootlace
2 fathoms	2 pieces of leather bootlace
3 fathoms	red bunting
4 fathoms	blue serge
5 fathoms	line with 1 knot
6 fathoms	tape
8 fathoms	leather
10 fathoms	line with 2 knots
15 fathoms	line with 3 knots
20 fathoms	2 pieces of line

Morse Code

A . —	N — .	1 . — — — —
B — . . .	O — — —	2 . . — — —
C — . — .	P . — — .	3 . . . — —
D — . .	Q — — . —	4 . . . . —
E .	R . — .	5 . . . . .
F . . — .	S . . .	6 — . . . .
G — — .	T —	7 — — . . .
H	U . . —	8 — — — . .
I . .	V . . . —	9 — — — — .
J . — — —	W . — —	0 — — — — —
K — . —	X — . . —	
L . — . .	Y — . — —	
M — —	Z — — . .	

Navigator's Checklists

Coastal

Steering compass with deviation chart

Hand bearing compass

Echo sounder and/or lead line

Distance log

Radio direction finder

Clock

Barometer

Binoculars, preferably 7 x 50

Charts

Tide tables

Pilot books

Light lists

Log book

Small notebook

Parallel rules or protractors

Dividers and pencil compasses

Pencils and erasers

Simple calculator

Weather forecast radio

Offshore

All items mentioned in the coastal checklist, plus:

Sextant

Chronometer

Nautical almanac

Sight reduction tables

Star charts

Plotting charts

All-wave SSB receiver

Radio stations frequencies guide

Bottle of champagne for first ocean island landfall

Phonetic Alphabet This is the recognized international phonetic alphabet:

Alpha	Juliet	Sierra
Bravo	Kilo	Tango
Charlie	Lima	Uniform
Delta	Mike	Victor
Echo	November	Whiskey
Foxtrot	Oscar	X-Ray
Golf	Papa	Yankee
Hotel	Quebec	Zulu
India	Romeo	

Power of Attorney, Example of for a Cruising Couple Here is the basis of a useful document for cruising couples to carry aboard their vessels, particularly when going foreign. It could help bypass some unpleasant bureaucratic tangles at a time of great stress. Have a document like this drawn up by your lawyer before you go cruising. If you draw up your own document, be sure to have it correctly notarized. (This example is based on a suggestion by Lin and Larry Pardey in *The Capable Cruiser*.)

POWER OF ATTORNEY

To whom it may concern:

I,_____, sole legal owner of the vessel _____, registered in_____, registration number_____, registered tonnage_____, do hereby solemnly swear that in the event of my death, incapacitation due to illness, or absence through any cause, determined or undetermined, it is my wish that all my rights and powers as owner and captain of the said vessel shall be ceded unconditionally to _____.

He/she shall have the right to operate the said vessel and make whatever arrangements he/she might deem necessary for its normal or abnormal operation, including shipment by road, rail or sea. He/she shall be empowered to place the vessel in storage or safekeeping, to leave the vessel and to return at will, without relinquishing any of the powers granted under this document.

He/she shall have the right to hire another competent captain to carry out his/her instructions. His/her signature shall, in the event of my death, incapacitation or absence, be accepted in the place of mine on any legal documents pertaining to the operation, ownership, and movements of the aforementioned vessel, under any and all national and international laws that might apply.

Take legal advice about how such a document should be signed, witnessed, and notarized.

Sound Signals, Most Common Rules 34 and 35 of the International Rules for Preventing Collisions at Sea, and the U.S. Inland Navigation Rules

Definitions Signals required by the International Rules differ in some respects from the signals required by the Inland Rules.

Both sets of rules, however, define a *short* blast as lasting 1 second. A long or *prolonged* blast lasts from 4 to 6 seconds.

Both define *whistle* as "any sound signalling appliance capable of producing the prescribed blasts" that complies with the specifications in Annex III of the rules.

Annex III gives technical details of frequencies required by vessels of different lengths. Basically, the bigger the vessel, the deeper the note; the smaller the vessel, the higher the note.

Most pleasure boats fall into the "less than 75 meters in length" range, which calls for a fundamental whistle frequency of 250 to 525 Hz.

For boats of less than 20 meters (66 feet), the whistle should be capable of being heard for at least half a nautical mile. For vessels between 20 and 75 meters (66 and 246 feet) the whistle should be audible for one nautical mile.

Bells must be made of corrosion-resistant material, and designed to give a clear tone. Aboard boats between 12 and 20 meters (39 feet 4 inches and 66 feet) in length, the diameter of the mouth must be not less than 200 mm (7.87 inches). Boats less than 12 meters in length may have smaller bells.

The mass of the striker must be not less than 3 percent of the mass of the bell, and you must be able to operate the striker manually.

When the rules mention an *overtaking* vessel, they refer to any vessel that is approaching (getting nearer to) another vessel from a direction more than two points (22.5 degrees) abaft the other vessel's beam. At night, the overtaking position is where you can see only the stern light of the vessel ahead and neither of her sidelights.

In daylight or any other time, if there is any doubt as to whether you are overtaking or merely crossing, you *must* assume you are overtaking and act accordingly.

If the vessel you are about to overtake changes course, you do not suddenly become a crossing vessel. Once designated an overtaking vessel, you remain so and you must keep clear until the other vessel is "finally past and clear."

It is important to note that where the rules refer to a *sailing vessel*, they are talking about the means of propulsion. If a sailing vessel with sail set is being propelled by auxiliary power, she is regarded as a power-driven vessel. A sailing vessel using auxiliary power with sail set must exhibit forward, where it can best be seen, a conical shape with the apex downward.

Under the Inland Rules only, boats of less than 12 meters (39 feet 4 inches) in length are not required to show this shape, but may do so. Also, it is not necessary to exhibit this shape aboard a sailing

217

vessel that is proceeding under power only, without the assistance of sail.

Maneuvering and Warning Signals (International Rules)

Meeting or Crossing

A power-driven vessel underway and in sight of another vessel, power or sail, must signal a change of course with short blasts of her whistle.

A sailing vessel is not obliged to signal a change of course.

One short blast means: "I am altering my course to starboard."

Two short blasts mean: "I am altering my course to port."

Three short blasts mean: "I am operating astern propulsion."

Note that these signals are not requesting permission, or confirmation that such maneuvers are safe. They are merely informing other vessels of the maneuver that is taking place.

Overtaking

When overtaking in a narrow channel or fairway, however, or in a traffic separation scheme, a vessel intending to overtake another (including a sailing vessel intending to overtake a power vessel) is required to ask permission by way of signals, and to receive confirmation, before she starts to maneuver.

Two prolonged blasts followed by one short blast mean: "I intend to overtake you on your starboard side."

Two prolonged blasts and two short blasts mean: "I intend to overtake you on your port side."

Before you overtake, the vessel about to be overtaken must signal her agreement by sounding the following blasts: one long, one short, one long, one short. That is the Morse code for C. (Or: Sí. You gettit, señor?)

If she regards the proposed maneuver as dangerous, the vessel about to be overtaken must respond with the danger or doubt signal, which is "at least five short and rapid blasts on the whistle."

Note carefully that the first set of signals covering a change of course in meeting or crossing situations is required to be made only by power-driven vessels. The second set (overtaking) is required of all vessels, including sailing vessels.

Maneuvering and Warning Signals (Inland Rules)

These rules apply only between power-driven vessels. Sailing vessels are not obliged to make these signals at all, and power-driven vessels are not required by the rules to make these signals for sailing vessels.

Meeting or Crossing

When two vessels are in sight of one another, and meeting or crossing within half a mile of each other, they must indicate their maneuvers with the following whistle signals.

One short blast means: "I intend to leave you on my port side."

Two short blasts mean: "I intend to leave you on my starboard side."

Three short blasts mean: "I am operating astern propulsion."

The other vessel must signal agreement with the first vessel's intentions. The way she does this is by repeating the signal. If she is in any doubt, she must sound the danger signal, whereupon both vessels must take all precautions to avoid collision until a safe passing agreement is made.

Overtaking

When a power-driven vessel intends at any time to overtake another under the Inland Rules (no mention here of narrow channels or fairways), she must first seek permission by sounding the following signals on her whistle.

219

One short blast means: "I intend to overtake you on your starboard side."

Two short blasts mean: "I intend to overtake you on your port side."

These are virtually the same signals as required under the International Rules, except that the preliminary attention-getting sign—two long blasts—is omitted.

If you become confused when you read that one blast means "I intend you leave you on my *port* side," as well as "I intend to overtake you on your *starboard* side," it might help to remember this simple rule of thumb: In all cases when meeting, crossing, or overtaking, your signal indicates which way *your* boat might possibly have to turn. One blast means your boat might need to turn to starboard; two, to port. Of course, although a turn is not always necessary, particularly when you have right of way, a signal *is*—and this helps you to remember what it is.

Once again, the boat to be overtaken must signal her agreement, this time by repeating the signal; and if she is in any doubt, she must sound the danger signal of five or more short and rapid blasts.

Approaching Bends

All vessels, power and sail, approaching a bend in a channel or river where they cannot see vessels approaching from the other direction must give warning of their approach by sounding one prolonged blast.

Any vessel within earshot shall answer with a similar signal.

The Inland Rules also say that a vessel under power (including a sailboat using its auxiliary motor) must sound one prolonged blast (4 to 6 seconds, remember) when leaving a dock or berth. That's certainly a rule honored more in the breach than the observance, and for obvious reasons. But if you, like most, choose to ignore it, just be very sure you don't collide with a passing vessel. The rule is very plain.

Finally, the Inland Rules state that none of this whistle business is necessary at all if you use your radio to call the other vessel and reach agreement about who will give way. You may still sound the signals if you wish, but you're not obliged to do so if you've made radio contact and come to an agreement.

Of course, in the unlikely event that you can't agree on the radio, the rules still require you to exchange signals "in a timely manner." Furthermore, the whistle signals shall then prevail.

What they're really saying is this: If you can make radio contact earlier than you would normally sound a whistle signal, well and good. But you may not, in attempting to make radio contact, postpone whistle signals beyond the time when they would normally need to be made.

Sound Signals in Restricted Visibility

Under the International Rules and the Inland Rules of the United States, these signals must be made, by day or night, "in or near an area of restricted visibility." The rules do not define *near* in this context.

International and Inland Rules

One prolonged blast, at an interval of no longer than two minutes, shall be made by a power-driven vessel making way through the water.

Two prolonged blasts (with an interval of about two seconds between them) shall be made at intervals not exceeding two minutes, by a power-driven vessel underway, but not making way through the water. (The definition of underway is "not at anchor, or made fast to the shore, or aground.")

International Rules Only

One prolonged blast followed by two short blasts, every two minutes or less, shall be made by:

- A vessel not under command
- A vessel restricted in her ability to maneuver
- A vessel constrained by her draft
- A sailing vessel
- A vessel engaged in fishing
- A vessel engaged in towing or pushing another vessel

It helps to remember that one long blast and two short blasts (dah-dit-dit) is Morse for D, and signal flag D means "Maneuvering with difficulty."

A vessel at anchor may give one short blast, one long blast, and one short blast (Morse code R) if she is at anchor unless she is a vessel engaged in fishing at anchor or a vessel restricted in her ability to maneuver and carrying out her work at anchor, in which case the signal would be code D, one prolonged and two short.

A vessel at anchor must also sound a bell, of course. The signal is 5 seconds of rapid ringing every 60 seconds or less. A vessel of 100 meters or more will, in addition to sounding a bell in her forepart, also sound a gong for 5 seconds immediately afterward in her afterpart. If she has all the whistles, bells, and gongs, you may be sure she is a vessel of some consequence.

Incidentally, the rules say that vessels of less than 12 meters (about 39 feet 4 inches) are not obliged to give any of the sound signals so far described. However, the rules go on to say that such vessels have to make "some other efficient sound signal" at intervals of not more than 2 minutes. It sounds like very much the same thing to me, and I'd advise you to make as loud and as conventional a noise as you possibly can.

A recording of the enraged roar of a frustrated

gorilla might be a very efficient sound signal, and one likely to attract and grip most sailors' attention. But the last thing another skipper needs to worry about in fog is strange jungle noises that might or might not mean danger. Let him know you're there and let him know what you are.

Inland Rules Only

One prolonged blast followed by two short blasts, at intervals of not more than 2 minutes, shall be made by:

- A vessel not under command

- A vessel restricted in her ability to maneuver, whether underway or at anchor

- A sailing vessel

- A vessel engaged in fishing, whether underway or at anchor

- A vessel engaged in towing or pushing another vessel

However, when a pushing vessel and the vessel being pushed ahead are rigidly connected in a composite unit, they are regarded as one vessel and give the signal for an ordinary power-driven vessel.

A vessel at anchor must ring a bell rapidly for about 5 seconds every 60 seconds or less; a vessel of 100 meters or more shall sound the bell in the forepart of the vessel and shall, immediately after that ringing, sound a gong for about 5 seconds in the afterpart of the vessel.

A vessel at anchor may also (not instead of) sound Morse code R—one short blast, one prolonged blast, one short blast—to give warning of her position to an approaching vessel.

As in the International Rules, boats of less than 12 meters (about 39 feet 4 inches) are not obliged to give these exact signals, but if they choose not to, or are unable to, they must "make some other efficient sound signal at intervals of not more than two minutes."

Tank Capacity in U.S. Gallons: How to Determine

L = length
H = height
R = radius
W = width

All measurements in inches
Cylindrical tanks
Gallons = (L x 3.14 x R x R) ÷ 231
Rectangular tanks
Gallons = (L x H x W)÷ 231

Tensile Strength of Materials Used in Boatbuilding, Approximate

In pounds per square inch

Pitch-pine	7,800
Oak	10,000
Spruce	10,100
Cedar	11,400
Lignum vitae	11,800
Douglas fir	12,400
Elm	13,500
Fiberglass (ordinary layup)	15,000
Teak	15,000
Ash	17,000
Iroko	21,000
Mahogany	21,800
Tobin bronze	22,000
Manganese bronze	30,000
Aluminum	40,000
Mild steel	60,000
Monel	75,000
Silicon bronze	80,000
Stainless steel	85,000
Kevlar	90,000
Graphite	170,000
Spectra	168,000

Tillers, Minimum Sections of

These are the approximate square-section sizes at the rudder head recommended for tillers of various lengths. From the rudder head, the tiller should gradually taper down to a comfortable hand-grip of 1.25 inches in diameter. The square section adds strength in a vertical direction to withstand accidental blows from gear and stumbling crewmembers.

Length (Feet)	Size at Rudder Head (Inches)
2.5	2.08
3.0	2.20
3.5	2.35
4.0	2.43
4.5	2.53
5.0	2.63
5.5	2.70
6.0	2.78
6.5	2.85
7.0	2.93
7.5	3.00
8.0	3.08

Useful Formulas and Conversion Factors

Areas

Circle: Radius times radius times 3.1416

Cylinder: Circumference times height plus areas of circles at ends

Ellipse: Overall length times overall width, divided by 2, times 3.1416

Parallelogram: Base times vertical height

Parallel trapezoid: Total length of the parallel sides, divided by 2, times vertical height

Sphere: Diameter times diameter times 3.1416

Triangle: Base times vertical height, divided by 2

225

Volumes

Cone: Radius times radius times height times 3.1416, divided by 3

Cube: Base times side times side

Pyramid: Side times height, divided by 3

Sphere: Diameter times diameter times diameter times 0.5236

Circles

Area: Radius times radius times 3.1416

Circumference: Diameter times 3.1416

Diameter: Circumference times 0.3183

Pressure

Average pressure exerted by the atmosphere: 14.69 pounds per square inch at sea level

Barometric: The atmosphere supports a column of mercury 29.92 inches high, on average, at sea level

Power

One horsepower = 746 watts of electricity = a rate of 33,000 foot pounds per minute

To convert kilowatts to horsepower, multiply by 1.341

Speed

To convert knots into miles per hour, multiply knots by 1.152

To convert miles per hour into knots, multiply mph by 0.868

Water: Weight and Volume of Fresh Water

One cubic foot = 7.481 gallons = 62.39 pounds

One cubic inch = 0.0043 gallons = 0.0362 pounds

One gallon = 8.340 pounds = 0.1336 cubic feet

One ton = 32.054 cubic feet = 2,000 pounds = 239.79 gallons

Weight for equal volume: Fresh water = sea water times 0.974

Water: Weight and Volume of Seawater

One cubic foot = 7.481 gallons = 64.05 pounds

One cubic inch = 0.0043 gallons = 0.0371 pounds

One gallon = 8.561 pounds = 0.1336 cubic feet

One ton = 31.225 cubic feet = 2,000 pounds = 233.59 gallons

Weight for equal volume: Sea water = fresh water times 1.027

Weather Proverbs Some of the oldest rules of thumb for forecasting weather at sea have been handed down as proverbs. Although we might scoff at one for being too trite, or another for being more suited to a fairy tale than to a serious weather manual, the simple reason for their survival over the centuries is that their advice has proved valid, and is still useful in a general sense. Tempered by a knowledge of local weather patterns, they often provide as accurate an indication of coming weather changes as many supposedly more sophisticated sources.

Quick rise after low
Oft portends a stronger blow

A falling barometer is a sign of an approaching depression. The strongest wind often does not arrive, however, until the barometer has begun to rise again. Furthermore, gales accompanied by a rise in pressure are usually more gusty and cantankerous than gales that arrive with a falling barometer. The average rate of advance of a depression is 17 miles per hour, and two to three days is a common time to pass over one spot. Secondaries might pass in 24 hours.

227

Mackerel skies and mares' tails
Make tall ships carry low sails.

> This is a reference to high winds aloft forming widespread cirrocumulus (clouds that looked as if they'd been scratched by a hen, according to the old-timers), indicating strong surface winds to come.

Red sky in the morning,
Sailors take warning.
Red sky at night,
Sailors' delight.

> Some experts offer scientific explanations for this ancient jingle, which may or may not apply. But most of us are content to accept the fact that it has simply proved highly reliable.

Rainbow to windward, foul fall the day;
Rainbow to leeward, rain runs away.

> Now this one is infallible, or pretty nearly. If the rainbow's to windward, then the rain must also be to windward, and if it isn't raining on you already, it's likely to soon. The opposite applies to a rainbow to leeward. Of course, your eyes could probably tell you all this without the need for an ancient rhyme, but what the heck: At sea it pays to have as many backup systems as possible.

A backing wind says storms are nigh;
Veering winds will clear the sky.

> Or, to put it another way:

When the wind shifts against the sun
Trust it not, for back 'twill run.

> This is largely true (in the Northern Hemisphere) of weather systems with a southerly component in their movement, although there is sometimes not much of a time lag between the change of wind and weather.

When halo rings the moon or sun
Rain's approaching on the run.

Another fairly accurate assessment. The U.S. Weather Service confirms that rain follows about 75 percent of sun halos and about 65 percent of moon halos. Most often, you're looking at the sun or moon through the ice crystals of lofty cirrus clouds. A sky filled with these indicates an approaching warm front and soft soaking rain.

When boat horns sound hollow
Rain's sure to follow.

This one doesn't ring with the veracity of a really ancient proverb, but it works just as well if you can figure out what *hollow* means. It's that certain special sharpness, that certain change of tone that occurs with changes in the moisture content of the air.

Beware the bolts from north or west;
In south or east the bolts be best.

Fairly obvious, this lightning guide, if you live in the north temperate zone where the weather usually travels from west to east. If you spot lightning in the northwest, it's probably a thunderstorm coming toward you. If it flashes south or east of you, you can probably wave it goodbye.

Finally, there will always be those who turn to the birds when all else is lost:

Seagull, seagull, get out on t' sand,
We'll ne'er have good weather with thee on t' land.

That's a British rhyme, of course, but seagulls seem to behave much the same the world over, scavenging at the water's edge when the weather sets fair, and scavenging on mankind's waste dumps far inland when it comes over foul. Regrettably, seagulls don't seem to be brilliant forecasters; they tend to be more *driven* by the weather than to *anticipate* it, so their usefulness to boaters is definitely limited. Personally, I'd rather rely on the barometer.

Weight of Rope and Chain: Approximate
Weight of 100 feet

Diameter (Inches)	Nylon Rope	BBB Galvanized Chain
¼	1.6	76
⁵⁄₁₆	2.6	115
⅜	3.8	170
⁷⁄₁₆	5.2	225
½	6.9	295
⁹⁄₁₆	8.8	350
⅝	10.8	430
¾	15.8	600

Weights of Some Common Materials Found in Boats (in pounds per cubic foot)

Aluminum, cast	165
Bronze	509
Cedar	31-55
Copper	554
Concrete	144
Cork	15.7
Fiberglass	96
Fir	32
Fir plywood	36
Ice	57.5
Iron, cast	450
Kerosene	51
Lead	712
Mahogany	35
Oil, diesel	53
Oregon pine	35
Spruce	27
Steel, structural	490
Steel, stainless	500
Styrofoam	1.3
Teak	48
Tin	462
Water, fresh	62.4
Water, salt	64

Wind Pressure According to Wind Speed
(in pounds per square foot of frontal surface area)

Area (sq. ft.)	Pressure (Pounds)			
	30 Knots	60 Knots	80 Knots	100 Knots
1	3	13	22	32
50	150	630	1115	1600
150	450	1890	3345	4860
200	600	2520	4460	6480

Wire Gauges, Non-Critical
These are the American Boat and Yacht Council standards for wire gauges for lighting and other non-critical purposes on a 12-volt system. All wires should be multistranded.

Current (Amps)	Length of Wire (Feet)					
	10	15	20	30	40	50
5	16	16	16	14	14	12
10	16	14	14	12	10	10
15	14	14	12	10	8	8
20	14	12	10	8	8	6
25	12	10	10	8	6	6

For 32-volt systems, add 4 to these gauges.

Wire Gauges, Critical
These are the American Boat and Yacht Council recommended wire gauge sizes for critical circuits in 12-volt systems, where a voltage drop may be no more than 3 percent.

Current (Amps)	Length of Wire in Feet (Source to Load)					
	10	15	20	30	40	50
5	14	12	10	10	8	6
10	10	10	8	6	6	4
15	10	8	6	6	4	2
20	8	6	6	4	2	2
25	6	6	4	2	2	1

For 32-volt systems, add 4 to these gauges.

BIBLIOGRAPHY

The Boatman's Handbook, Tom Bottomley. New York: Hearst Marine Books, 1984.

The Capable Cruiser, Lin and Larry Pardey. New York: W. W. Norton & Co., 1987.

Celestial Navigation for Yachtsmen, Mary Blewitt. Camden, Maine: International Marine, 1994.

Chapman's Piloting, Seamanship, and Small Boat Handling, Elbert S. Maloney. New York: Hearst Marine Books, 1989.

The Complete Book of Anchoring and Mooring, Earl Hinz. Centreville, Maryland: Cornell Maritime Press, 1986.

Cruising Under Sail, Third Edition, Eric C. Hiscock. Camden, Maine: International Marine, 1986

Getting Started in Powerboating, Bob Armstrong. Camden, Maine: International Marine, 1990.

Heavy Weather Sailing, Adlard Coles. London: Adlard Coles Ltd., 1970.

A Manual for Small Yachts, R. D. Graham and J. E. H. Tew. London: Blackie & Son Ltd., 1946.

The Nature of Boats, Dave Gerr. Camden, Maine: International Marine, 1992.

The Practical Pilot: Coastal Navigation by Eye, Intuition, and Common Sense, Leonard Eyges. Camden, Maine: International Marine, 1989.

Psychology of Sailing: The Sea's Effects on Mind and Body, Michael Stadler. Camden, Maine: International Marine, 1988.

The Rigger's Apprentice, Brion Toss. Camden, Maine: International Marine, 1984, 1992.

Sail Power, Wallace Ross. London: Adlard Coles Ltd., 1973.

Seaworthiness: The Forgotten Factor, C. A. Marchaj. Camden, Maine: International Marine, 1987.

Sensible Cruising Designs, L. Francis Herreshoff. Camden, Maine: International Marine, 1973, 1991.

Singlehanded Sailing, Second Edition, Richard Henderson. Camden, Maine: International Marine, 1988.

Skene's Elements of Yacht Design, Francis S. Kinney. New York: G. Putman's Sons, 1973.

The Small-Boat Skipper's Handbook, Geoff Lewis. London: Hollis & Carter, 1977.

Spurr's Boatbook, Upgrading the Cruising Sailboat, Second Edition, Daniel Spurr. Camden, Maine: Seven Seas Press, 1991.

Stapleton's Power Cruising Bible, Sid Stapleton. New York: Hearst Marine Books, 1992.

Traditions and Memories of American Yachting, W. P. Stephens. Camden, Maine: International Marine, 1981.

Voyaging Under Sail, Eric C. Hiscock. London: Oxford University Press, 1959.

The Way of a Ship, Alan Villiers. New York: Charles Scribner's Sons, 1970.

Yacht Cruising, Claud Worth.

Yacht Designing and Planning, Howard I. Chapelle. New York: W. W. Norton & Co., 1971.

The Yacht Navigator's Handbook, Norman Dahl. London, Ward Lock Ltd., 1983.

The Yachtsman's Pocket Almanac, Gary Jobson. New York: Simon and Schuster, 1986.

The Yachtsman's Week-End Book, John Irving and Douglas Service. London: Seeley Service & Co. Ltd., 1938.

233

INDEX

235

241